CAPITAL DISRUPTION

THE STORIES OF NINE PIONEERS AND THEIR VISION TO CHANGE THE LENDING INDUSTRY

DUDLEY K BEYLER

Chicago, IL

Nothing in this book should be taken as investment advice. Information published in this book has been prepared for general information purposes only. If you are considering investment, please consult a financial advisor before taking any investment action.

Capital Disruption: The stories of nine pioneers and their vision to change the lending industry

Published by BlogIntoBook
222 W Merchandise Mart Plaza
Suite #1212
Chicago, IL 60654
www.BlogIntoBook.com

ISBN: 9781619847552
eISBN: 9781619847569

Printed in the United States of America

For bulk orders contact admin@laveercapital.com

Special Thanks and Acknowledgements

THE MARKETPLACE LENDING ecosystem is a *pay it forward culture*. I continue to be the beneficiary of many who helped craft this book. I am also one of many sharing this story. This is a book about the founders and people of influence in this space. I thought the story would best be told by those who are creating it. This is why I setup the book as a series of interviews. My intent is shaped by my observations and experience. The book's goal is awareness and education.

In Memory of Nathan Popkins –
February 21, 1979 – July 30, 2017

Nathan was tragically taken from us shortly before this book published. Nathan was a friend and business partner. My heart breaks for his family, friends and teammates at Align Income Share Funding.

I always looked up to Nathan and enjoyed our many conversations ranging from Align to baseball. I often told people if you wanted your brain to hurt, have a conversation with him. His thoughts were never surface level. He always played deeper.

I met Nathan as he was launching Align (then named Cumulus). I had the privilege of being one of the first buyers of the income share agreement he was originating. I can still see the smile on his face when we agreed on that first deal. The smile was different than his traditional goofy smile. I never asked, but my guess is behind that smile was his level of pride in what he was building and his ability to convince others the value he was creating. I think only an entrepreneur can understand the high. *Nathan will always have that feeling and I will always remember that smile.*

You will find Nathan's interview in this book. The Align team continues to work to fulfill the vision Nathan courageously set out to achieve. He was a pioneer. He doggedly pursued the path less taken.

Align has a strong team. Naturally, good leaders attract great talent. I have no reservation the Align team has their heads down executing his vision. Somewhere Nathan is proudly at peace with his spreadsheets. His spirit lives on.

Contents

My Journey

I WAS TWENTY-SIX AND became my own bank. Or so I thought. I made my first unsecured consumer loan on a marketplace platform.

It was 2008 and I began investing in this nascent concept of peer-to-peer lending. The first companies at scale in the United States were Lending Club and Prosper. Both focused on consumer unsecured lending. (Think of consumer unsecured lending like you would a credit card.)

On the surface the concept was simple. Credit-worthy borrowers were paying rates of interest on their credit cards that I, as an investor, would like to earn. Who has not looked at their credit card and said, "I wish I earned that rate when the bank is paying me 0%"? For the first time, a non-institutional investor could.

Typical loan sizes at the time were $12,500-$17,500. A borrower's reason for credit was refinancing higher interest debt, education, medical and home remodel. A lender could lend a minimum of $50 toward the total amount borrowed.

As we came out of the financial crisis and the economy began to grow I noticed changes in marketplace lending. I recognized I was bumping into more sophisticated hedge funds, private lenders and family offices. As this continued, I observed rates begin to fall as the competition to buy loans increased. During the financial crisis the Federal Reserve reduced rates to

0%. Early adopters were seeing this fledgling asset class as an opportunity for yield.

While I still liked the consumer lending opportunity, the relative rates were not as appealing based on the risk I perceived. At this time I began looking for alternatives in the marketplace lending space. I found similar platforms originating small business loans at rates that were significantly higher. I researched a few platforms and even made a couple loans. I never went further. I personally struggled to define and understand the risk.

At this time, I realized an investor's ability to categorize the risk, like a consumer unsecured loan, generated a sense of homogeneity. The unsecured consumer lending platforms were grading credit (e.g. A, B, C, etc.). If credit was perceived as standardized, then the risk scoring became almost formulaic. For me to achieve the best returns, I needed to find a market where assigning a credit grade did not exist.

In the late summer of 2014 I found a couple nascent platforms funding single family home real estate loans. The concept of real estate lending resonated. I had, on paper, a claim on a real asset. With each loan I received an independent appraisal of the property. After the crash, I knew firsthand with other investments how the appraisal pendulum had swung from loose to tight. I liked how I could search the property on Google Maps and view it. I thought the historical pricing for the home and area was valuable. I found other data sets interesting like area income levels (affordability), comparable rents, property days on market, inventory versus sales (turnover) among others. In short, there were many methods for me to vet a property. Single family real estate is a difficult market to homogenize, thus reduces probability a platform could quickly become a manufacturer of financial product.

From the fall of 2014 through the summer of 2016 I made numerous real estate based loans. The outcome was exceptional. The overwhelming majority of loans have since been repaid. Weighted average days outstanding for loans paid in full were 210 days. When assuming conservative rates of returns on the few defaulted notes, the interest earned is 8.95% (annualized yields based on 360 days/year). The average weight of each loan in the portfolio was 1.51%. This level of diversification was intentional.

Finding Dissent

I thought this was interesting and I began sharing my experience with local Chicago banks and other investors. The response I received was surprising. Investor response was binary. They either thought it was compelling, asked questions about my experiences and followed up or they thought this space to be a bomb ready to explode. For investors, there was no middle ground.

While I thought the banks would be slow to come around I quickly found most were unaware these marketplaces existed or responded with, "Yeah, I have heard of Lending Club/ Prosper, but not exactly sure how it works." Ironically, I was having parallel conversations with community/regional banks about their challenges finding quality loan flow, declining foot traffic in their branches, skinny net interest margin (the spread of how much interest a bank charges borrowers and pays you on your deposits) and increasing expenses related to increased regulation.

As my conversations grew I continued to hear themes like "a loan needs to be consummated with a handshake" and "computers cannot judge character." To me this was strange. It reminded me how at one point Amazon was a small retailer of books and how I bought my compact discs (CDs) and rented movies from Blockbuster.

The behavior reflects a behavior I had observed already once in my career. My background is trading commodities, interest rates, currency, equities and volatility. I have traded on the Chicago Mercantile Exchange, Chicago Board of Trade, Intercontinental Exchange, New York Mercantile, Eurex Exchange and Chicago Board of Options Exchange. Not too long ago the "trading pits" held all the trading volume, screaming, fighting, spitting and wrestling in an attempt to execute the best order. While fun, it was inefficient. Yet many tenured "pit traders" insisted the only way to trade was in a pit. Many believed humans were better than computers. I witnessed guys wiped out by the technology change in a matter of months. I witnessed others who grabbed the opportunity and built a fortune. It happened fast and the impression left was indelible.

Banking's Kodak Moment?

I began to wonder if the lending market was in a similar transition. Despite advantages, were banks losing touch with their customers? Were these new tech-focused participants taking market share?

As customers moved online, vast branch networks, once a strength, became a major liability. Customer acquisition costs were too high and customer lifetime value was in decline. Borrowers showed little brand loyalty with traditional lenders. For over a hundred years, banks acquired customers by opening a neighborhood branch then waited for customers to bring deposits and one day finance their mortgages. Comparatively, platform companies have experimented with digital customer acquisition funnels.

Banks have some of the lowest net promoter scores (customer

acceptance). There is a running joke that millennials would rather visit the dentist than a bank. Consider the differences in the lending process:

Process	Banks	Platform Lenders
Application	Paper heavy, multiple requests	All digital
Data Collection	Paper, branch-focused, some digital	API-based, big data
Decisions	Manual, Email/Fax	Automated review
Ongoing oversight	Manual	Digital monitoring

At its core, we are observing a conflict between old and digital operating models. Old operating models believe information technology (IT) is a cost center while digital believes IT is a driver of growth. Old operating models rely on people, whereas digital is data driven and soon enhanced by artificial intelligence (AI). The old model avoids risk and thus aims to maximize efficiency. New digital models emphasize flexibility and responsiveness.

To illustrate, consider the following example of direct channel acquisition: In the fall of 2015, OnDeck announced a partnership with Intuit. Intuit owns QuickBooks, one of the most popular small business accounting software packages. Together they announced a $100 million small business lending fund. Small business owners would have the opportunity to use QuickBooks data to apply for a loan. While a bank will ask a business owner to submit paper financial statements, OnDeck will digitally qualify the candidate on transaction-level detail. This partnership allows the lender to manage and measure ongoing performance trends. This powerful acquisition channel is a great method to price and track the lender's risk. While a bank currently monitors the borrower, it is largely manual.

To be sure, I am a centrist in the bank/lending platform argument. I do believe banks and lending platforms have their respective strengths and need each other.

I have summarized the relative strengths and weaknesses of each:

Platform Lenders	Banks
High cost of capital	Low cost of capital (deposits)
Ease of customer experience	Antiquated and poor customer experience
Technology/data talent rich	Challenged to attract tech and data talent
Uncertain regulatory environment	Stable regulatory environment
Millennial-focused business	Poor use of digital channels
Lack of capital reserves	Legacy technology
Scarcity of customer data	Conservative use of data
Lack of physical distribution	Culture of "No!" / Inflexible

Industry convergence pressure is in two parts. Part one: increased regulatory burden and associated costs create incentives to scale. Part two: technology has a history of winner take most. Concentration seems inevitable. It is the path to this convergence that is unclear. As platforms focus on profitability, instead of pure growth, and become accretive to an acquirer, then a wick is lit. Alternatively, in some scenarios I see a platform(s) as the hunter.

Opportunities for Borrowers and Deal Sponsors

There are parallels with other disrupted industries and opportunity provided in these marketplaces for investors, small-medium business and real estate deal sponsors. For example, the entertainment industry is notorious for barriers destroyed by those creating unique content and using digital channels to distribute. In the past one needed a record label or a network TV executive to determine "air time." Today there is no invitation. Permission is not asked.

In the past small business equity and debt investment was limited to the immediate network of the entrepreneur. Real estate sponsors raised capital from their private networks and, if lucky, commercial banking relationships. Platforms are democratizing opportunity. No longer are deals exclusive to the "country club." Who are the small- and medium-size business operators that will use this channel for growth capital and expand their business? Who is the real estate sponsor who builds a real estate empire with limited partners organized by a marketplace?

One can look at this as an opportunity or a threat. While there will be differences between the future of finance and other industry, the potential impact should not be discounted.

Risks of writing a book like this

I am aware of the risks writing a book like this at this early stage in its life cycle. Platforms have failed and more will fail. There will be bad public relations and mistakes. I can guarantee it.

Waiting is a large and willing herd anxious to say "I told you so!" I have already had people question my intent for this book in light of the 2016 industry challenges. Guess what? Wells Fargo had a bad 2016 too.

The industry is moving fast and will look a lot different in twenty-four months. The credit market will look different. From a macro level, credit markets the past several years have been benign. When, not if, the credit cycle turns there will be losses. To be fair, banks are not immune to failure in a down credit cycle. Our society does not need to be reminded that banks start and fail. Failure with lending platforms may be more pronounced as they lack government-backed deposits. This supports my theory for bank and lending platform consolidation discussed earlier.

Despite the risks, it does not mean platform lending is ineffective and valueless. Earlier I referenced Amazon. At the turn of the century the "dot-com crash" shook out a lot of weakness and over time Amazon has prevailed in changing the face of retail. Although many did, discounting the future of e-commerce at the time would have been an oversight.

The stories

I believe the marketplace lending story is compelling and has legs. So I reached out to founders and influencers in the space and asked them to share their stories. I think you will find the stories of their journeys amazing.

- After struggling to get credit for his business, Sam Hodges, his partners and team built Funding Circle.

Since 2010, Funding Circle has lent more than $3 billion to over 25,000 small- and medium-sized businesses.

- Nav Athwal, Founder of Realty Shares, was a real estate deal sponsor, broker and lawyer who recognized the lack of capital efficiency at the sub-institutional level. He set out to fix this and has since executed over $500 million in real estate transactions.

- Denise Thomas, Founder of Apple Pie Capital, has a family history in the franchise business and inherently understands its financing challenges. Apple Pie is quickly becoming the "growth engine" of the franchise industry and recently secured a $180 million loan purchase agreement providing committed capital for their clients.

- Frank Rotman and his partners at QED took a credit card spinoff out of a regional bank and built what is now known as Capital One. They since left Capital One, founded QED and funded fintech companies, now with billion dollar valuations, at their earliest stages.

- Nathan Popkins was an investment banker who identified an opportunity with a nascent funding idea called an income share agreement. After vetting his theory, Nathan left his job and founded appropriately named Align Income Share Funding.

- Jorge Sun was one of the founders of OnDeck Capital who left to found LendingFront and bring tech to non-tech savvy banks. LendingFront allows a bank to originate loans online that is competitive in user experience with tech-focused competitors.

- While working in the U.K. Krista Morgan grew frustrated with forex and other related banking fees when sending money back home. She thought a peer network would be a superior and more cost-effective solution and spun the idea into a receivables financing business.

- During the real estate crash Jason Fritton observed sophisticated participants buy properties at significant discounts. Jason thought the opportunity was limited to few and set out to expand access to capital for these assets.

- Peter Renton sold his printing business and began to invest in Lending Club and Prosper loans. As Peter learned more he saw a parallel with his prior business and built a blog into a brand and global conference across three continents with thousands in attendance.

I was thoughtful in selecting these founders and influencers. I wanted to reflect the breadth of the market and the diversity of thought and experience. Note the commonalties causing action. The stories of humble beginnings, market acceptance and subsequent growth are inspiring. I trust you'll enjoy reading the interviews as much as I did putting this together.

Sam Hodges:
Co-Founder, Funding Circle

www.fundingcircle.com

F UNDING CIRCLE'S GROWTH has been extraordinary since its founding in 2010. Funding Circle has originated more than $3 billion worth of loans and helped over 25,000 small businesses gain access to credit. Amazingly their investor base is over 60,000 retail and institutional investors globally.

Although on a torrid pace, Sam believes the industry is still in the early innings. As you will read, Sam believes small ticket commercial lending, in the US, is badly broken. He claims Funding Circle has built a better model for three types of stakeholders: (i) borrowers, (ii) investors and (iii) the system.

When looking at where Sam and Funding Circle is today, I thought the convergence of his experiences— especially as a small business owner—was not a coincidence for his inspiration.

Dudley: Looking at your background—starting in fund
           management, Second Market, the fitness gym that
           led to Endurance Lending and eventually Funding
           Circle—can you talk to your evolution? Presumably
           "N" number of years ago, you didn't wake up and
           say, "Oh, small- and medium-sized business lending
           is what I'm going to do."

Sam: Your assumption or hypothesis is absolutely spot
           on. The decision to start what was then Endurance
           Lending Network, which today is Funding Circle's
           US arm, really was a culmination of two things. The
           first were a set of experiences that I and my then
           business partner, Alex Tonelli, had in building up
           a set of fitness businesses actually. He had worked
           at Summit Partners in Boston. They owned Snap
           Fitness, which was a franchisor of gyms, and saw
           the kind of unit economics and returns you can get
           in that space, so started a franchisee.

           I partnered up with him, invested some of my
           own capital, and what was really shocking was
           [that] despite the fact the business was actually
           working out quite well, it was really hard to get
           credit. We talked to equipment finance companies,
           we talked to banks, we talked to SBA (Small
           Business Administration) lenders; we talked to
           all sorts of different folks who theoretically were
           in the businesses of lending money to good small
           businesses. In each case, we were told one of three
           things.

           Either, "You're just too small. We just don't do
           this. You're turned down." Or, two, "We're going

to drag you into a,"—they wouldn't say this, but by experience is what it ended up being—"drag you into an interminable process where you have to spend months and you have to fill out your balance sheet in triplicate by hand, and we'll maybe let you know in ninety days as to whether you might be eligible." Or, number three, for some of the non-bank players: "We'll give you credit, but we won't tell you how much it costs. We won't actually be able to produce an amortization schedule. We can't calculate the APR, but just trust us."

The more we kind of proceeded through that, the more we realized small, very small ticket commercial lending, in the US, is very badly broken.

The other, and this is kind of the second thread of it, was I knew from my time at Second Market that there was a whole universe of investors who were really excited about the prospect of being able to put capital into non-traditional assets, ones where they could actually get really interesting outsized risk adjusted returns. ELN, what is now Funding Circle, really was the culmination of those two realizations.

Fast forward from kind of that moment of realization, which was roughly June 2011, from that point until summer of 2013, we built up the business, went and raised equity, lined up lending capacity, built our team, built our initial product, and along the way got to know some folks from the UK who were basically doing the same thing. They were operating from fundamentally a similar moment of realization. Samir [Desai], Andrew [Mullinger], and James [Meekings], who were the founders of Funding Circle company in the UK, were . . . university friends. They all worked in financial services; they'd looked at this problem through a couple of different lenses and basically just came to the same realization.

After getting to know them and really seeing a lot of common purposes strategically as well as kind of cultural affinity, we decided to put the businesses together. Came to terms on that in August of 2013, announced the deal in October of 2013, and have been running it ever since.

Now, today, Funding Circle is the leading global lending platform for SME (small and medium-sized enterprise) credit. We've originated more than $3 billion worth of loans and helped over 25,000 small businesses get access to credit. We have over 60,000 retail and institutional investors globally operating in four countries and have almost 650 employees.

Dudley: In terms of the loans, can you talk a little bit about what a loan looks like: term, line of credit, interest only, all of the above, your range on rates, your amortization schedules?

Sam: Our product range in the US—and it's pretty similar in the other four countries where we operate— we do term loans one to five years, interest rates starting at 5½% and going up through the mid-20s. On the low end, it's basically a replacement for a bank loan. It's quite equivalent to what community banks, particularly, used to do in the space. Then, as you move up, you move out from a credit risk perspective and out in term, the pricing looks more like what you'd get with a credit card, with a big difference being you can pay it back over multiple years. It's an installment product.

Amortization is very straightforward. It's just straight-line amortization. If you actually take our rates and turn it into an effective APR, you're talking about, in all cases, we stay under 36% APR as a hard and fast cap, but in most cases, you're talking about a high single digit or teens APR.

Dudley: In terms of your borrowers, are you industry agnostic? Are you B- to B, B to C?

Sam: We're quite broad from an industry perspective. The way we think about this is really three-fold. One, we think that most forms of smaller businesses are not particularly well served in this capacity. If you can build out this capability, you can apply it to different industry and geographic verticals.

Second point I'd make is a lot of the same disciplines from a credit and risk assessment process applies regardless of what the industry is. That's not to say we don't sensitize our model with, with industry; we do. That's something you absolutely need to do well in order to kind of think this through. The fundamentals are very, very similar.

Then, thirdly, our thought is that being a marketplace, it makes sense to try to serve all types. As we have a wide range of different investors, we also want to serve a wide range of different borrowers. For investors, having that breadth means that we are, in effect, offering, you can almost think about it as the beta return of SME credit in the US. It's a great way to get direct access to what is a really important part of the, of the household sector from a, from a fixed income returns perspective.

Dudley: You mentioned the fundamentals parallel from industry to industry, but can you drill down a little bit more on the underwriting and how you look at the different industries that may have different levers, seasonalities or management execution risks?

Sam: A lot of this is just driven by now the range of data that we've built up over the last six years. At its core, we are analyzing the business first. We are taking a look at firmographic information, age of business, size of business, location, industry. We look at the financial characteristics of the business: leverage ratios, financial operating ratios; we look at the amount of liquid assets; we look at basically all the financial gearing of the business; and we look at trends.

We analyze both bank statement data as well as tax return data, both from an analysis and a verification perspective, to understand what is the financial momentum of that business. At the end of the day, what the models— our credit decision models—do is really pull in all that information, parse it and depending on our view on certain elements, weight different factors against each other to ultimately come up with an appropriate credit decision and price.

Dudley: What's your average loan size?

Sam: Our average loan size is about $120,000. Range, like I said, is between $25K and $500K. A typical borrower for us is a business that has been around for seven or eight years that is looking for, like I said, $120-$130,000, that has over a million dollars in revenue, that has either more employees and that is looking for expansion capital of some form. That might be money to remodel a storefront. It might be some mix of working capital and expansion of a new product line. Could be potentially acquiring a competitor. We have some flexibility on the use of funds dimension, which is I think one of the reasons why our product is so attractive.

Dudley: When I speak with regional community bankers here in the US and talk to them about this kind of channel in terms of sourcing loan flow, they come back to me and say, "Look, it's important for us to look the customer in the eye and shake their hand, because that's a part of the vetting process." What do you say to that? How do you counter that? Presumably, the primary part of your vetting is algorithm based.

Sam: I guess what I would say is two-fold. One is, certainly, character. You know, someone's willingness to repay and their commitment to the business is an important signal. I guess, what I'd argue is, humans have proven again and again that they're okay at making those decisions, but they're not actually great at it. If you can build a large data set, you can actually come up with a much more refined informed view of that. Moreover, you can also think about, how do you trade off different factors against each other?

We don't think small business credit should be one size fits all. The reality is, sure, there are plenty of banks who do small business lending, but more or less, it's one size fits all. You either qualify for the core product or you don't. If you do qualify, the spread in potential rates is very small. We, again, just think that you're excluding a whole addressable universe of small businesses that are very strong and very credit-worthy. You just need to think about how to do that risk-based pricing well. The simple fact is, and we have data to prove this, a human alone is not very good at making that decision.

Dudley: When we talk about the banks, a lot of banks are reluctant to give cash flow-based loans. They're looking for more assets, where you are cash flow loans. How do you get comfortable with the security and what are your recovery rates like?

Sam: I just want to say we look at, again, both assets and cash flow. At the end of the day, what we're trying to understand is: What is going to be the probability of default of the loan and of the business. What our model parses is a lot of the same information that one might look at if you're doing cash flow-based lending or asset-driven lending. We just have that kind of internally calibrated in the way we approach it.

In terms of security, you're absolutely right. We file a UCC on the business. Oftentimes we are the senior secured lender, and what that does is just provide us a level of safety or comfort that should things go wrong, the borrower will at least be cooperative with us in doing the workout and recovery. From a collections perspective, collection rates vary a lot by industry and, and type of business and so forth. I guess, what I'd say is, the range is anywhere between calling the low end 10 to 15% up to in certain parts of the business, in the UK, for example, where we really have it nailed as an art, our collections levels are actually north of 40%.

Dudley: Industry to industry, how would you compare that to some of the other folks in the space?

Sam: What I'd say is given the type of loan that we're doing and the fact that we're lending out to more established businesses, even if they're not asset-intensive businesses, typically this isn't something where the business just evaporates overnight. Typically, even if something does go away, we and the entrepreneur expect, generally, there is something left. Certainly you get some goose eggs, but in most cases, you can figure out a way to work with the borrower.

Dudley: What do these borrowers look like? What does their balance sheet look like and their debt equity mix, if they have debt, or is it pure equity?

Sam: It varies industry to industry. It varies entrepreneur to entrepreneur. It varies in business maturity. I mean, again, one of the things that our model allows us to do is kind of not have simple rule-based ways of doing all that. Instead, we factor in all those different factors, and it means that the potential acceptance box that we have is I would say, almost certainly wider than what a bank is able to do, just based again on the maturity of our data set.

Dudley: If you're financing expansion capital as opposed to working capital, how do you look at the growth and the potential growth that your expansion capital is going to add and how that impacts the payback and how quickly that could happen for security on your loans?

Sam: As a general rule, we're not lending on a speculative basis. We need to see a business with a clear way of paying back the loan based on their current operating model, revenue and margins. This isn't something where we're betting on, "Oh, it's going to be a J curve, and if they spend this $200,000 properly, maybe in two years we'll get our money back." Because it is a fully amortizing product, we need to have real visibility into ability to repay as soon as the loan is funded.

Dudley: When I have conversations with banks, they say, "Look. It costs me the same to underwrite a $50,000 loan as it does a $1.5 million loan." When your average loan is $120,000, and you talk about going lower than that, are you creating a new category, are you replacing somebody or are you filling a void and it's not necessarily a new category? How do you look at this?

Sam: Well, I think it's kind of all of the above. On one level, I guess we could say—in terms of what banks used to do—remember our banking system used to be a lot more fragmented than it is today. If you go back twenty years, there were close to 19,000 independent depositories. Today, there are closer to 6,000, 6,500, somewhere in that range.

That's been driven by smaller bank closure; it's been driven by consolidation in the space, and it's, in part, being driven by a heap of ongoing compliance costs that make it hard for banks to be in certain lines of activity. Some of those direct operating expense hits. Some of them are capital charges. Because, obviously, if you're a bank and there's moral hazard because you're taking in deposits and you've got to comply with Dodd-Frank and Basel III, a lot of cases you can hold a decent amount of capital against certain assets that you acquire.

We—because we're not using deposits, because we're not a bank, we're not doing maturity transformation (borrowing money on shorter timeframes than they lend out)—we don't have those costs. We certainly are regulated, but it's just a fundamentally different form of regulation, and it works much more as an investment or securities business than it does like a bank.

Now, in addition to that, we also have an advantage with regard to cost to acquire and cost to process. That's really where the technology aspect comes in. We used certain technology on the front end to deliver a really high quality borrower experience, and we also use it as a way to very efficiently do the information on-boarding and processing necessary to be competitive in this category.

Dudley: Can you discuss, very generally, your funding sources? You mentioned you have a peer element, partial loan, whole loans and institution participation. I assume you have your own credit facilities as well in terms of the balance sheet?

Sam: No. We, we don't use our balance sheet other than to take true lender risks during a period of time when we originated the loans. We'll typically hold loans in the US on our balance sheet for a few days. We have taken a state-by-state licensing approach, so we are actually the lender of record. We think there are a lot of advantages to having this model, and then, after we've taken that true credit risk, at a certain point we have a set of institutions, fractional investors, as well as managed fund vehicles that then invest in those loans through us.

Basically, the way it works is, we have several dozen institutional buyers who typically buy whole loans, we have both accredited investors and other institutions that are buying fractional, and then we have two private funds in the US as well as a listed investment trust that we listed on the LSE (London Stock Exchange). Actually, if you want to see it, it's FCIF.L. It's currently trading above par, which we're very proud of. It was about a $230 million vehicle when we IPO'd it a little under a year ago that's a source of liquidity on the marketplace as well.

Dudley: What keeps you up at night? About this, at least. Keeping it contained to this.

Sam: Yeah. I've got a three-month-old at home. She keeps me up at night occasionally.

So on the business front, I guess what I'd say is, I don't think, there's nothing that existentially keeps me up at night. It's a complex business in a very big, fragmented market, and so figuring out how you can scale under those conditions, that's certainly hard. I'm really proud of how the team has kind of rallied around that, and I'd say we take a very mission-driven approach to what we do here.

Our mission is to build a better financial world, and I think we take that really seriously in terms of delivering a great borrower experience, but also in terms of making sure we have really delighted investors who are excited about the asset class that we're building here. Lots of operational headaches, but nothing existential keeping me up at night.

Dudley: If there's a hiccup in peer or direct lending, do you think there's any contagion risk within the space, even not related to you but people backing off in general?

Sam: I think there's still a lot of confusion around what the space is and what are the differences between the different players, and I think that just reflects the fact that it's so reasonably nascent in so far as financial services businesses go. When I hear contagion, I think 2008-2009 financial crisis, of which I had a pretty up close personal view. I don't see a way that something like that could happen in our space, particularly, but you're not talking about crazy counter party risk, you're not talking about maturity transformation, you're not talking about Wall Street getting drunk. Those conditions just simply don't exist this time.

That being said, I think from a reputational perspective, when one player hiccups or takes a misstep, certainly there is blow-back and additional scrutiny on the entire space. That's something that, I think, certainly we as a space need to be mindful of, and that's also why we and a number of other players have started really focusing on building out responsible practices standards.

We—Prosper and Lending Club—formed the Marketplace Lending Association here in the US to develop industry standards in the space. We, in the UK, are a charter member of the Peer-to-Peer Finance Association. [In] both of those major geographies, we've taken a really proactive stance, kind of getting ahead of where we anticipate issues might occur and making sure that we are, as much as we can, living up to the very high standards.

Dudley: What's your crystal ball forecast for where you are, how you grow and evolve over the coming years? I won't hold you to it.

Sam: Just in terms of what the major kind of drivers of growth would be or . . . ?

Dudley: Drivers of growth, new opportunities, or is the industry so fragmented that you can just continue to scoop and consolidate?

Sam: I think we're still in the early days. It's hard to gauge, but for a nine-inning game, I think we're probably in the bottom of the third, maybe the bottom of the second. There's still a lot, a long way to go just in terms of building market awareness of, of what we're doing. I think we've proven out that we can find great borrowers, we can do the credit assessment, and then there's certainly capital supply available for the asset class if you can figure out the right product and distribution for it.

            We think that there's going to be both, kind of using a simple concept, both intensive and extensive growth. The intensive growth is we're going to get a lot better at doing what we do today— doing borrower acquisition costs effectively and processing loans in a really efficient way. We're also delivering a great borrower experience. We get better at that every single quarter. We have a lot of metrics that show that. We, on the extensive side, are going to be looking at additional geographies and also additional product categories.

We think that small business lending is pretty badly broken in pretty much every market we've seen. So it's really just a question around how do we take the core capability we've developed here and extend it very thoughtfully so that we can serve a wider share of the market?

And, and what I'd add is, you have to remember, we're playing in absolutely massive market opportunities. I mean, SME credit in the US is a $250 billion a year origination opportunity, and there's somewhere between one and two trillion in outstandings. It's a very, very large market.

Dudley: That's where I think this is story gets really exciting.

Sam: There are some big secular trends that I think are driving all of it. Bank de-levering is a big piece of it. The fact that rates everywhere remain very low, negative in, in certain parts of the world. I think we don't need a super low rate environment to be successful. It does help. It just makes it even easier for this product to stand out as a really attractive asset from a fixed-income perspective, and that increasingly is how a lot of our investors are seeing it. Where else can you get a mid-to-high single digit with not a huge amount of credit volatility from a returns perspective?

Dudley: That's a great question.

Sam: I meant it as an open-end question, which is: I don't think there are very many places where you can find those returns, and we're one of the few places, which is why I think you're going to continue seeing a lot of, a lot of excitement around the asset class.

Dudley: When you listed on the LSE, I think that's interesting because there seems to be this bifurcation between public and private markets. Those that can participate in private markets, going to what you said earlier about Second Market and what you recognized, there seems to be a lot more opportunity to get those returns through your vehicle and others, but now that you're bringing it to the public markets, that's a compelling opportunity.

Sam: We agree, and we've gotten really strong both institutional and retail uptake. Again, I think, the first platform to directly go to market with something like that. The reception has been very favorable. I think there are a number of opportunities to expand on that front as well.

Dudley: Is there a story or a message that you want people to understand that's a priority for you?

Sam: I'd just close by saying we really think this is better than many models that have been used to form credit in the past, and it's better for three different types of stakeholders. It's better for borrowers because it's more efficient, it's fair, it's fast. For investors, it's better because there's less intermediation, there's more access to return; you can build a diversified portfolio credit risk. We think that's really exciting.

We also think that it's actually better for the system. That goes back to we're not using deposits; there is not a maturity transformation; you don't have moral hazard. From a policy perspective and from a communications perspective, it just remains really important for us to make sure that we are messaging on that clearly and people really understand what the space is all about.

Nav Athwal:
Founder, Realty Shares

www.realtyshares.com

Nav founded RealtyShares in 2013 and has since executed over $500 million in real estate deals on its platform. This comprises nearly 1,000 investments, with multiple properties per investment at times. Nav believes platforms like his will fundamentally change real estate financing similar to how Uber and AirBnB changed the way we travel.

More than $80 million in principal has been returned to investors. This has given confidence to investors, and they have responded by increasing investment size and frequency. About 80 percent of the platform's active investors are high net worth individuals investing in seven to eight deals per year.

Nav believes the strongest founders set out to try to solve a challenge they have encountered themselves. As a broker, deal sponsor and real estate attorney, Nav worked on his own deals as well as client deals and large institutional deals. He observed how efficient real estate capital is at the institutional level and inefficient on the sub-institutional level. He created RealtyShares with the goal of eliminating these inefficiencies to make real estate as easily investable as buying or selling publicly traded stock.

Dudley: What is RealtyShares?

Nav: RealtyShares is an online marketplace for real
            estate investing. We connect a growing number of
            investors, both individual and institutional investors,
            to private real estate opportunities through our
            marketplace. These are being offered by real estate
            companies and professional real estate operators
            that are buying commercial or residential assets,
            either to hold them and generate rental income or
            to buy and flip them and generate a yield over a
            short duration. The RealtyShares marketplace helps
            connect these two stakeholders. It allows them to
            transact much more efficiently and also provides an
            access point that didn't exist before. There was no
            comprehensive marketplace where you could invest
            in deals and access different opportunities and
            different markets. The RealtyShares marketplace
            is really the first attempt to create efficiency within
            the real estate investing world that doesn't exist
            today. Also, [RealtyShares is] making each part of
            the transaction easier, streamlined and more tech-
            enabled.

Dudley: You mentioned it hasn't been done before. You're
            trying to create these efficiencies and connect these
            parties. It is my understanding, your background
            was as a real estate attorney. What were some
            of the moments where you thought, "There's
            something here. There's this huge void. I think we
            can fill it or I think we can put some technology
            behind it." Can you walk us through the idea
            generation stage?

Nav: I spent over a decade in real estate prior to founding
            the company, in a few different capacities. I started my
            career in real estate brokerage, actually, where I was
            helping buyers acquire small apartment buildings,
            single-family homes and some commercial assets. I
            was working with smaller operators that were very
            local and were buying smaller buildings that were
            typically $10 million or $15 million dollars. I then
            transitioned into real estate law, where I was working
            at a big law firm in San Francisco. There, I worked
            with large institutional clients like public REITs and
            private REITs including Equity Residential, Avalon
            Bay on much bigger deals.

            I think the "aha" moment behind [realizing]
            RealtyShares could really have some teeth came in
            the inherent differences within two types of real
            estate deals. On one hand, you had the institutional
            deals, plenty of capital efficiency, plenty of capital
            availability and a lot of foreign and domestic capital
            chasing these large deals. On the small cap side, the
            deals I was doing as a broker, there was just a lot
            less efficiency and a lot less institutional demand
            for those deals. Because of the size of these deals,
            it didn't make sense for an institution to deploy
            capital. It just didn't make sense from an efficiency
            standpoint. How inefficient it is relative to the
            institutional size deals is really what prompted the
            idea in the first place.

            As a real estate investor, broker and lawyer, real
            estate's something that's near and dear to my heart. I
            also started my career as an engineer, so I understand

what technology can do to make a process much more efficient and make doing business much more efficient. Seeing the end-to-end transaction process as a broker and as an attorney, I realized just how much inefficiency there was in that transaction process and how much inefficiency there was in the small cap deal in terms of raising capital. This is really what prompted the idea for RealtyShares. What we're driving is creating capital efficiency and efficiency in how folks invest in the small cap commercial real estate world.

Dudley: You have this hypothesis and this concept. How did you go about testing it? Before you made that leap or maybe you made the leap and then tested it. Can you just walk us through how you tested it first?

Nav: For the first six months of the business I was still employed as an attorney. It was more of a concept stage. It was more white boarding, really thinking through the challenges and the business model. Could this work? It was really more of an ideation stage for us, and it was really just thinking through the challenges and getting excited every step of the way. We were building something - creating something we were so passionate about. We knew there was a need for it. Eventually, when you're starting a company, you just have to do it. You talk to customers and have something for them to look at and talk about and give feedback on. For us, it's a two-sided marketplace. With any two-sided marketplace there's this challenge of where do you start first? Do you start with the supply and deals, or do you start with the demand and capital?

Without the deals, it really didn't make sense to engage with capital because we didn't really have anything to engage them with. Given my background in real estate, I was able to leverage my network and find a few early deals where I had folks who were strong real estate operators that were willing to take a look at this sort of marketplace approach to raising capital. By leveraging that network and using some early PR, content and blogging, we were able to acquire our first set of investors. The process in those first few transactions was pretty much done offline from the money transfers to the document signings. We were even sending things by mail, which is obviously much different than it is today. Those first few deals, it was really like, let's see if there's something here. Let's see if people trust an online platform enough to say I want to invest in a real estate deal using technology.

This was in late 2013, so yields were pretty much nonexistent. Folks were looking for yield, and we had a really good yielding product within the real estate world. I think that really helped investors say, "Normally, if the interest rates were higher, if bond yields were higher, maybe I wouldn't look at this, but they're so abysmal that I need to earn yield." Investors were willing to take a leap of faith. I also think another thing that really helped was just the shift to online investing and online money management that we've seen over the last five to ten years through different platforms like Lending Club. Even before that, with E-trade and Scottrade, and now the robo-advisers through Betterment and

Wealthfront. I do think there's this shift towards online investing, online money management, lower-cost investing, cutting out the middle-man, cutting out the intermediary and generating better yield. I think that is influencing a lot of the traction of online platforms like RealtyShares and others.

Dudley: You're going through that process. You have your MVP (minimum viable product), you have the deal, you're very hands-on at that point. What was the moment, or do you recall a moment specifically where it was like, "We have something here?"

Nav: I believed we had something even before we launched the first deal. I was thinking about my time trying to raise capital for deals or trying to find good deals to invest myself. I always felt like we had something, but when I felt like it was real was when we funded our first two deals. We launched our first two deals pretty much simultaneously. We had no anticipation of, "Is this going to succeed or not?" We had never done it before. When we started seeing activity and people show interest by clicking a button in the deals, that was when we were like, "Okay, there's customers there." The initial conversations were by phone. I remember taking phone calls and talking to investors that were interested, and helping explain the platform to them and seeing their interest and passion in what they were doing.

Their enthusiasm for the platform is really what made me excited. I knew this was something that was going to be very interesting and something that's needed, but now there's some validation. As a startup founder, you're so close to your company and your idea. Sometimes you forget reality, but this was reality telling me, "This actually could make sense." I think it was after I saw that initial interest in the deals and in the platform. When I called these folks, the conversations ended up being real. I think that's what really drove me to say, "Wow. This could be really exciting." Shortly thereafter I actually quit my job and went at it full-time because I felt like there was some early validation, and it was something I wanted to pursue.

Dudley: Lending Club started roughly six or seven years before you. Why do you think the first platforms have gone from consumer unsecured lending to real estate? Real estate is something that is more tangible, and people can relate to easier, more broadly speaking.

Nav: Let me start with that first part on why did the early platforms like Lending Club and Prosper go after consumer. I think there are two elements to that. Anytime someone's starting a company or a business model, I think the strongest founders are the ones that are trying to solve a challenge they themselves have experienced. They've been in the shoes of at least one type of customer within their business model. When you learn about Renaud Laplanche's background – he's the founder and former CEO of Lending Club – you realize why he went consumer.

He was his customer. He was someone who was paying an exorbitant amount on club credit card interest rates, and realized that he came from technology and also the securities side, because he was a lawyer. He was trying to solve a problem he himself was experiencing. I think the model a company chooses, at least the companies where there's a founder that could potentially lead the company to success, is based on the solving their own problems and own dilemmas. I think that drives what shape the business ends up taking.

Beyond that, I think the consumer problem is a little bit easier on one hand. Real estate's a great asset, but there's also a lot of moving parts in a real estate deal. You don't just have someone's FICO. You're not just dealing with a person. You're dealing with a person and an asset, so there's just a lot more involved. I think when Lending Club was started in 2006 the real estate market was so overvalued. This was right before the crash. Finding good deals or being able to take advantage of dislocation in the market, it didn't really exist back then. Money was fast and loose. Prices were quickly appreciating, and there was the complexity of the underlying asset itself. I think that probably drove folks away from real estate at that time, and really drove them towards the easier assets like the consumer. After that, you saw small business lending. Small business lending is obviously a little bit more challenging than consumer, but easier than real estate in a lot of ways.

I really think it's probably a combination of those few things that drove the early platform folks on problems other than real estate. I think once you see the validation in these other models, in the consumer and small business lending space, and you see the sheer size of the real estate market, the application of these models to real estate just makes a lot of sense, albeit with challenges, because there is a tangible asset. They're challenges that we think are very much solvable, and we're working towards solving [those] every day.

Dudley: One of the things that I think is really interesting about RealtyShares is you're on all parts of the capital stack. You have debt. You have equity. Can you talk to that a little bit in terms of the strategic element behind it?

Nav: Early on, when we were thinking about, "What is this company going to stand for? What are we really building here? What are we trying to allow people to do?" We decided that we wanted folks to be able to raise capital more efficiently for their deals. We have this big gap in the capital markets for small cap real estate deals. Those are deals that, obviously, are too small for institutions to deploy capital into directly. We want to open up capital access to quality operators that have good deals. On the other hand, we're thinking about the investors and we started looking at just case studies of some of the most successful investors out there. The Harvard and Yale endowments came to mind. They generated very significant yields. 20 to 25 percent of their portfolio has been allocated to real estate.

The first part of what we were trying to do from the investor standpoint is create an ability to diversify into the real estate market, create an ability for individual investors to invest in real estate as easily as if they were investing in the stock or another publicly traded security. Beyond that, I think we also thought, "Real estate is this massive market. Diversifying into real estate's fine, but what about the asset class in general?" There's so many opportunities. There's short-term opportunities, long-term opportunities, commercial, residential and multi-family. There's debt. There's equity. For us, it was really about, how do we create [the] ability for this to be a marketplace where you can diversity into real estate, but also across different types of real estate?

Couple that with the fact that we really wanted to provide a type of capital for our borrowers and sponsors that we thought was very inefficient offline. We identified two opportunities. One was commercial equity. Commercial debt is relatively efficient offline, but equity is pretty much nonexistent. It's really friends and family capital that's being used for that equity component. On the debt side, where we saw a gap was [in] bridge lending, short-term loans where banks weren't providing access. There were these very expensive hard money lenders coming in and providing access, but at a really expensive cost to capital. It was a combination of wanting to provide ability to diversity in and across real estate, but also focus on those areas where that capital is the most inefficient. That led us to create a marketplace that focuses on both debt and equity and commercial and residential. I think that helps form why we ended up going as broadly as we did. It's really to service our customers better and create a better marketplace experience.

Dudley: Regarding deal terms, what can an investor expect to see on the platform with an equity-related deal? I realize there's a range of deals and debt-related deals, but if you could just speak generally to where investor expectations can be?

Nav: On the debt deals, most of our deals were on the single-family side. That can be anywhere from a one-unit, a single-family detached residence up to a four-unit or a four-plex. Most of our deals on the debt side have been just that single unit detached single-family home. That's typically a six or a twelve month duration loan. There's a monthly interest payment, and that interest can range from anywhere from 8 percent on the low end up to maybe 12 percent on the high end. The pricing depends on our credit model and where the risk falls of that specific borrower and deal.

We rolled out a commercial debt product in the last year, given the success of the single-family product and it has been very well received. We were the first platform to offer commercial financing across the full capital stack. Typically, they're going to be a multi-family asset with five or more units, or a retail asset where there's really a bridge loan investment that could be anywhere from 12 to 24 months. Both have similar yield characteristics, but are backed by a commercial asset rather than a single-family asset. All of these are first-lien secured. They're all backed by a trust, mortgage or deed of trust that's secured in the first position. That's the debt product we offer today.

On the equity side, we offer two types of products. We offer a preferred equity product and a JV equity product. The preferred equity product functions similarly to debt in that it's typically behind a first-lien debt instrument but has priority over the sponsors and their LP investors' equity in the deal. It's like a mezzanine position. Obviously, a higher yield than the first lien, because it's in a riskier position in the cap stack, but lower yield than the JV equity product when you're in the last position in the cap stack. That's typically a 12 to 36 month product, not secured by the asset but secured by the membership interest in the LLC that owns the property. The yields there are typically going to be 12 percent on the low end up to maybe 15 or 16 percent on the high end. That's typical in a commercial asset on the platform today.

The final type of product is our JV equity product. It's a very similar asset type as the preferred equity, but a different cap stack position because you're in a JV or common equity position rather than the preferred equity, which means you're at a riskier position in the cap stack. Your yields are going to be a lot higher though, so our yields there typically start at a 14 percent internal rate of return, and could go up to a 20 percent IRR. There are different types of cap stack positions, assets and return profiles based on a level of risk that the investor wants to take. What we often see is a lot of investors want to put money into all of these yields and build or diversify their portfolio, going back to the statement I made before about diversifying across real estate. A lot of them will put some money in the debt products, the first-lien debt, some in preferred equity and some in JV equity. All the risk investment return is still in the low single digits but is backed by a lot of different opportunities across different markets.

Dudley: Your investor base, is it accredited, non-accredited, family office, institution?

Nav: When we first kicked off the platform, all of our investors were individual, accredited investors. Most of our investors are still that base, and that's something that's held true for the last two-and-a-half, three years since the business has been in existence. We started there because of the pure retail investors that are non-accredited. It was really hard to go after them initially because of regulation. We wanted to start in a place where we weren't going to have to go through a very expensive regulatory process to be able to open the platform, because we obviously wanted to be very lean and test the model before putting in a lot of resources and raising a lot of money. We didn't go after institutions immediately, because we didn't have a track record. We thought that would also be an uphill battle. We started with this quasi-retail investor because there's a lot less of them in the general population, but they're also a lot less regulated.

I would say about 80 percent of our capital is still coming from that base of investors. They love the platform and invest typically seven to eight times across any given year. The average investment they're putting into a deal is going up over time. We're seeing a lot of positive cohort trends amongst that base. Over the last six to eight months, we started broadening that to institutional investors. Now we have hedge funds, family offices and registered investment advisors using the platform as well. We see that number growing, so we think the liquidity breakdown is going to continue to grow in the favor of institutions because we're seeing so much more demand than we did when we were first kicking the platform off. For me, it's always been about capital markets, or cap liquidity diversification.

I think Lending Club did this really well, where they had a base of institutions but also a really strong base of retail individual investors. We want to do that at RealtyShares. We really want to create a marketplace where you can have different investors coexisting so you're not overly concentrated with any one type of investor. They also give you the ability to continue offering additional types of financing products, because each investor is going to have their own demand in terms of risk and returns, and that will translate into an ability to fund different types of companies and product types. For us, institutional capital expansion is a priority, but we also don't want to lose sight of the retail investor and the individual that really is an important sticky base of capital for our platform, and is going to be important into the future as we continue scaling the company.

Dudley: When you look at these deals, how are you underwriting them? How are you measuring risk in context of the deal and the sponsor?

Nav: For us, we have about a 2 percent selection rate. Out of 100 deals, about two will be accepted onto the platform. It really starts with the sponsor quality. When we're looking at an application that comes to us, and now we're getting thousands every month, the first thing we look at is who is the sponsor? How many deals have they done before? What is their financial and background history? Is this someone we want to do business with? We're underwriting that sponsor before we ever touch the deal. You can have an amazing real estate asset and an awful sponsor. We're just never going to do that deal, because the challenges of managing investment real estate require sophistication.

We're really plugging into internal and external data sources to test and validate track record, background and credit, prior deals and performance on those deals. That's a combination of our data source as well as our underwriting investments team that looks at each deal and every sponsor to get comfortable with it. We also do reference checks that are typically on the sponsor. We'll want to call a bank partner or a former managing partner that did business with the sponsor to really get comfortable with the relationship and how well they can manage a third-party relationship.

Once we get comfortable with the sponsor and their background and track record, then we look at the deal. On debt and equity, we're trying to gather as much data on the asset as possible. That includes an appraisal, an environmental report and a title report. We're typically looking at a pro forma financial model. That's particularly the case for commercial deals that are multi-family. We're looking at whether the IRR or the yields that the sponsor is projecting in their model are achievable. That really requires us to test the assumptions around cap rates and vacancy rates, and get comfortable around those assumptions. That, again, is a data exercise, so there's some automation there.

Obviously, we're trying to increase that as well, as we have our underwriting team that's looking at every deal and looking at all the assumptions and stress testing them. The process is pretty involved. It takes us 25 days from start to finish for a new sponsor to really get them through the funnel. On the single-family side, it's quicker. It's usually 10 to 12 days. With technology, we hope to cut both of those timelines in half over the next 12 to 24 months, but there's still a lot of work involved in looking at an asset, underwriting the asset, getting comfortable with the sponsor and the asset, and then listing it on the platform for our investor base.

Dudley: The portfolio performance thus far, I realize some
           of the equity, probably still trying to realize what
           those returns have been, but can you speak to how
           it's gone? Defaults? Recovery rates? Number of
           loans?

Nav: We've now done nearly 1,000 different investments
           in the portfolio. A single investment may be one
           property or it could be more than one property,
           or it could be a fund, which could have dozens
           of properties. Thousands of properties have been
           funded through the RealtyShares platform in over
           nearly 1,000 separate investments. We've seen about
           40 percent of the portfolio go full-cycle, but with our
           deal volume increasing, that can vary significantly
           each quarter. That means deals that have been
           funded, the payments have been made, and the
           deal has been exited by the sponsor. We have seen a
           pretty robust exit percentage of our portfolio, which
           is great, because it provides data for new investors
           to look at to say, "Wow, RealtyShares really over
           performed here, or may have underperformed
           there." I think that's really good and it's a positive
           sign that the platform is working and that we're
           picking the right borrowers and sponsors.

           Generally speaking, without giving specific
           numbers, our portfolio has done very well, relative
           to a lot of other investment options out there. A
           majority of our deals have either performed as
           planned or, in some cases, over-performed. There's
           been slight underperformance on some asset classes
           and types. One thing that's unique about a platform

like ours is we educate both our data models and our investments team based on prior performance to make our underwriting better. For example, it's both sponsor and deal-based. If a certain asset class or a certain market we feel is underperforming or over-performing, we want to take that into account when underwriting future assets in that market. If a sponsor that we've worked with in the past does a really good job managing the asset or does a poor job managing the asset, then we'll take that into account when looking at a future asset with that sponsor.

We want to continue learning how deals are performing. Not only do we originate on the front end, but we look at the deal's underwriting and get comfortable with them and fund them. We also do the asset management function, so we're continuing to collect data on the asset post-funding. We're able to really know, "How is this market doing? [Are] the cap rate assumptions correct? Are the vacancy assumptions correct?" Then, [we] educate our underwriting team and data models around that. I think the portfolio generally performs very well. We're very excited about that.

Obviously, we've been in a relatively benign part of the real estate market, so the real test will come when there's a correction, and we think we've done a good enough job underwriting and looking at deals with the viewpoint of not only today's climate but also where the climate could be in 24 to 36 months. I think it's been great. We've been able to earn yield and generate yields for our investors that they aren't going to see elsewhere, especially if they're putting their money in bonds or their bank account or even in the S&P where there's a lot more volatility.

Dudley: You didn't mention certificate of deposits. I am heartbroken.

Nav: And certificate of deposits.

Dudley: The sponsors that have recognized what you're doing and jumped on early, what impact has it been to their business? Is it just another channel for them, or is it changing materially the way they conduct their business?

Nav: I think there's definitely early hints of it changing the fundamental way they do business, but I think right now what it's done is made raising capital for them almost like an [afterthought]. Before, raising and circling capital was really consuming their day-to-day. Finding a great deal is definitely one aspect of it, but making sure you can acquire that deal and you have the resources to do so is an important aspect of being a successful real estate investor. I think a lot of sponsors, myself included when I was doing my own deals, spend a lot of time thinking about where they can circle capital and having to have a conversation with these 10 to 15 LPs to get them comfortable. They think, "I have to prepare material. I have to do this, and I have to do that." That distribution channel is very inefficient. It wasn't a single distribution channel. It was multiple different conversations and is time-consuming.

I think one thing we've been able to do is bring a lot more efficiency into the capital-raising process for these companies. Even if they had an existing base of investors, that base of investors is not going to be as efficient as RealtyShares. Sponsors will come to us and say, "You've made raising capital for me an afterthought. It allows me to focus on the deal. It allows me to focus on running the right numbers and the models and really translate and do better performance for my investors, rather than spending 60 percent of my time talking to investors about raising capital or the deal itself." I think that's definitely apparent, and has happened.

In the future we hope to help our sponsors continue to do business better, not only on the capital-raising side, but also on other elements of the transactions. If we can help them be more efficient with the title and escrow process, we'd love to get involved there and provide value. If we can help on the purchase and sale process, we'd love to get involved there. Right now the focus is on how we help them get capital more efficiently. We want to be able to positively affect the end-to-end transaction process for them. We'll continue adding value, and hopefully, fundamentally change the way they do business for the better.

Dudley: How does this get off-track? Is there something that keeps you up at night in terms of a risk?

Nav: I think it's clear to me and it's clear to our backers and investors that this is now an execution play. There is a model here that's going to scale and there's customers that love the model. We're allowing folks on the investor and sponsor side to do business better by putting their money to work in a more lucrative way. Can we execute this without running into pitfalls that could derail us? I think of the few things that I think about in running the business is one, making sure we're hiring the best team to execute. A very important element of my job as the CEO is making sure the talent is there, and is driving towards a common mission and vision, without being derailed or defocused. That's very important.

A second element is definitely the market cycle. Real estate is cyclical. What I think about is less along the lines of our portfolio performing because I think we've done a good job underwriting, and more about what is the capital market's environment is going to look like and if there is going to be enough liquidity in the market. I think that's why I mentioned the diversification of our capital to make sure that we are thinking about investors that are broad enough, or even if there was a correction and some capital pulled out of real estate, that there would still be enough capital for us to continue growing the business in a down cycle. Obviously, you know, 2010, 2011 and 2012 were some of the best times to buy real estate, but a lot of capital was out of the market. It's unfortunate that capital comes back when the market's overheating again, but that's just the nature.

Dudley: That's how it happens, right?

Nav: That's the nature of the beast. The third thing is balancing the marketplace. With the marketplace model, you have this constant supply and demand piece. Where do you put resources? Where do you allocate resources? How do you create this equilibrium where you're not constantly out of balance? We're always thinking about resource allocation. Do we want to go allocate more resources to the sponsor side? Do we want to spend more marketing dollars there? Do we want to spend more marketing dollars on the investor side? There's this constant give and take that we're doing. I'm always thinking about what the more important driver is to the marketplace's success. It's always thinking about that balance. That's a critical component of what I do and what the team thinks about on a daily basis.

Dudley: I can't go without asking your crystal ball forecast for RealtyShares in particular, but the industry as well. You just surpassed the $500 million [mark], which is fantastic. I see that being small. I don't mean that in a negative way, but small relative to how big the real estate space is and how early innings this is for you. Can you talk about your crystal ball?

Nav: I admit, we're small compared to the market, but that's what's exciting.

Dudley: I think it's really exciting where you are. You've accomplished a lot. It's such a big market.

Nav: That's what's exciting. We feel like what we've done is pretty great. We've grown quickly. The team is very excited about what we've been able to achieve, but obviously, we're tiny compared to the overall market. We're barely scratching the surface area. We've seen good growth in our company, and there's so much more growth to be achieved. That's what really gets me excited about the massive market opportunity in front of us.

I think that's what's really exciting. In terms of the future what we're really focused on right now is continuing to add value to the marketplace. I think that starts with continuing to improve our underwriting capabilities, automate the components that allow us to be more quick or efficient, and continue to improve the delivery of capital process for our sponsors, all while also continuing to introduce tools for investors, both on the individual and institutional side and adding to our base of capital. Ultimately, our ability to scale over the next 12 to 24 months or even six months is really going to be based on how many deals can we look at, underwrite and put on the platform, and how much capital there is to invest in those deals. Bringing more efficiency to both sides.

On the deal side, I think we have a lot of deals coming to us. We are thinking about how to get to the best deals more quickly. How do we cut those 25 and 14-day timelines in half? On the capital side can we bring more capital and more liquidity to the marketplace so there's enough liquidity to fund the deals that we're listing? Those are the two things that we're really focused on.

We're narrowly focused on the sub-institutional market. That's where we want to stay focused. That's 50 percent of the total transaction volume, in terms of commercial real estate in the US. It's a big part of the market. We want to continue to add additional products. We are providing this bridge loan product on single-family and equity on commercial. I mentioned we're beta testing this commercial debt product. These sponsors and borrowers that we're doing business with are very, very sticky. They're asking for more products. They're asking for other types of financing. Over time, we want to be able to introduce other layers of financing products that can help them do business [and] that can add to the lifetime value they have with our marketplace. We're always thinking about how to add more value to our customers on both sides.

Five years from now I really see RealtyShares being an end-to-end transaction management tool for real estate that goes beyond just the financing piece and raising capital, to the purchase and sale, and the title and escrow. I think that's where we could go. In terms of our industry, I think real estate, marketplace lending and real estate crowdfunding, are all related but all different businesses. I think they're all interrelated in this online investing and fundraising realm. I think that the industry has grown pretty rapidly over the last seven to 10 years through platforms like Lending Club and SoFi. Real estate's a relatively new vertical. It's still trying to make its name in that world. It's a big, massive market opportunity, but still very nascent.

We saw a lot of platforms get created in 2012, 2013 and 2014 to tackle this problem. I think we're going to see some consolidation. We're going to see a few platforms lead the pack and really start taking a market leadership. I think RealtyShares will definitely be at the forefront of that. I think it's going to be really incumbent on those leaders to make sure that they're thinking about the industry and not just their own platforms. I think one thing that's important to remember is, we're still early adopters in an industry that there's a lot of incumbents that don't necessarily want us to succeed or may see it as a threat to their business. I think it's always going to be important to think about the industry and how best, from a branding standpoint and a growth standpoint, to build our businesses and think about not just our own platforms but the industry in general.

I think there's exciting times ahead for the online lending and online crowdfunding space, but there's still a lot of work to be done. There's still a lot of building yet to be realized. It's exciting. It's a challenge, and I couldn't be happier to be leading the charge here at RealtyShares.

Dudley: Is there a message that you want to get across?

Nav: I think the overall message is behavior. Investor behavior and how folks are thinking about their business and how they do business is changing. People are looking for better and easier ways to do business, and less friction in how they live and run their lives, including their investing activity.

We've seen the shift with platforms like Airbnb, Uber and Warby Parker that are just delivering a better product cheaper or more efficiently, or in a more frictionless way. Investing is obviously a tricky piece, because there's a lot of emotion there when you're investing your money. I think a similar shift is happening there, where folks are looking for more value for the fees they may be paying, or they're looking to pay [fewer] fees. We've seen a lot of platforms exist and get created for the very purpose of being a better or cheaper way to invest your money into X, Y, or X.

I think online investing and online lending and fundraising is here to stay. I think there's obviously challenges, because we're inventing new businesses within existing regulatory frameworks that weren't developed under the internet world. There are challenges, but I think it's exciting, and I think more people need to pay attention to it. I think there's ways to coexist even with existing players like banks.. We've seen a lot of banks use platforms like Lending Club to put money to work. I don't think it's necessarily going to kill the banks or kill the incumbents, but I think it's very important for folks that may not be in the industry to pay attention and learn about these industries because it is going to change fundamentally how we do business, just like Uber changed the way we call a car and get from Point A to Point B or how Airbnb is changing how we live in cities or how we travel when we're gone for business.

I think there's a lot of excitement around online investing and fundraising, but I think there's still a lot of education as well. We're excited to be able to educate and help in any way we can. I think your book will be a perfect tool for that as well.

Dudley: Thank you for the plug.

Denise Thomas:
Founder, Apple Pie Capital

www.applepiecapital.com

APPLE PIE RECENTLY secured a $180 million loan purchase agreement. This agreement provides committed capital for Apple Pie borrowers. Apple Pie is becoming the "growth engine" of the franchise industry. Apple Pie has not gone without notice as it boasts some deep-pocketed institutional investors like Fifth Third Bank.

Apple Pie's median borrower has over $2 million in their bank and greater than a 750 credit score, yet they are willing to pay higher interest to Apple Pie because working with bank lenders and the Small Business Administration is a pain point.

Denise has family history in the franchise business and she inherently understood the importance of quality of brand and borrower to reduce credit risk. She combined her knowledge of bringing product to market with her understanding of a franchisors need for capital.

Dudley: What is Apple Pie Capital?

Denise: Apple Pie Capital is a growth engine for the franchise industry. We are the first and only online lending platform that serves the franchise industry. Our product is primarily a lending product today but our future is much bigger than that. If you look at the franchise market, it's probably globally over $120 billion when you combine equity and debt. In the US, an area that we began to focus in initially, it's a $30 billion debt piece of the market annually. It's a large market. Some people call it a niche. It's a big niche of the small business segment, and counts for 3% of the GDP, and one in fifteen working Americans are in the industry, so it's huge and it really touches the economy in a big way. Always has, and has been a growing industry even through the worst of times. This industry has grown by 3-5 percentage points annually.

Dudley: Most marketplace lenders focus on small business and medium-sized business very broadly. Why did you choose to focus on franchises specifically?

Denise: I chose franchise for a couple of reasons. One, when I was looking at this space—and I actually got my inspiration while I was engaged in another asset class and market making business—a company called Colchis came to visit us. They talked about a fund of blended assets between the loans from Prosper and Lending Club that they were buying in a fund that they had marketed. That really intrigued me because it was an alternative to a bank. I saw how this was sort of wedging in and disrupting and creating a greater efficiency and a win-win for the consumer, et cetera. I didn't see anybody doing that in the small business arena, and there's a good reason for it. You saw back in that day the OnDeck Merchant Cash Advance product, but really nobody was funding new business units.

When I looked at that, I said there's a good reason. It's very fragmented; how do you know what Joe's Pizza Shop on the corner's revenues should be and how can you assess a business plan in terms of what the potential payback of a loan would be? That's something banks have had to do for years. How do you do that more efficiently? I worked backwards from needing an organizing principle for scalability. You'd have to have a scalable way to analyze, assess, monitor.

That led me to franchise for a couple of reasons. One of my key early advisors, as I was developing this idea, thought about franchise, but also my family has been an equity investor in Supercuts for over twenty-five years and also one of my family members owned a large area for Mail Boxes Etc., before it sold to UPS. I saw the quality of people that were buying into franchise over the years and I saw the profits and the process of many, many years through recession and all. I saw how brands stood the test of time if they were good concepts.

I began researching that. I had no idea how large that market was at the time, but it checked all the boxes in terms of scalability because a franchise has unit economics that are published. The federally regulated documents that franchise brands are required, by the Federal Trade Commission to disclose to consumers buying franchises, define exactly what they should expect from the unit economics of that business. It will vary by geography, but plus or minus it's a good baseline from which to assess people's business plans when building new units. Of course when you are in our business we're doing both recaps (recapitalizations), refis (refinancing) and new units.

We're able to see the performance history through data; both proprietary data provided by the franchisor and the model we've created to bring data in from other sources. We've been able to analyze and get a fix on what [the] likely performance is of a particular brand's units, which allows us to lend more confidently with a two-layered underwriting model.

That's really how I got into it. I didn't know if there was a problem with finance in franchise so I researched that for six months by going to a network that I had and interviewing brands and finding out what their issues were with funding and growth. There was a consistent cry for a better solution. That's how I ended up doing that combined with the fact that my personal background has always been in technology and financial services and or healthcare, both regulated industries, so I'm a bit of a serial masochist and I'm not afraid of difficult-to-crack codes in terms of taking chaos and making it orderly and using technology to leverage and create scalability.

I love doing that and that was just the perfect marriage between, I thought, a large market, a need and my skillset in building channels from scratch and creating inroads with new products and services. It's been really, really fun.

Dudley: Serial masochist, otherwise known as entrepreneurship, right?

Denise: Yes!

Dudley: You mentioned you have some history with your family in the franchise business. You mentioned the fund that was amalgamating Lending Club and Prosper loans. You've had some various leadership positions in finance and healthcare. How does that come together to lead to Apple Pie? Can you walk me down that path? Was it "Eureka!" or was it a gradual crescendo if you will?

Denise: Yeah, it morphed over time. I was looking at the larger small business space but I did not see a way to do that with good unit economics for a business like ours because of the fragmentation. When you can go into a channel—and I'll give you an example from my past. I was involved in the healthcare industry, a company called Navigenics that did genetic testing, personal genomics as it was named. It was a Kleiner Perkins Sequoia-backed company and I did the go-to-market strategy for that product and, really, the channel through national employers and also through physicians.

Now I'd never marketed through employers or physicians before. I'll take that back, I had marketed through employers but not as much. I learned a very important skill that I didn't know was unique and that is how to open a channel, build it, distribute a product through it, and service through it scalably, meaning they do the marketing and the distribution for you. I've done that in my career a lot as it turns out. The basis of that is building relationships, which take time so you have to be in it for the long haul. It begins with trust at a corporate sponsor level and then making it easy for them to rollout to the channel, in this case, franchisees. Doing that in a way that people trust in your product and your service.

That is what I refer to as B-to-B-to-C, the "C" being the ultimate consumer who is consuming your service. In this case, it's a borrower/franchisee. In the other case it was an individual who wanted to find out what they were predisposed to from a disease perspective and prevent it. It's understanding the whole value proposition and understanding the marketing channel and how to develop that cost effectively. The basis of our business, if you look at the franchise side or the investor side, it's really building relationships and trust through your actions and delivering what you say you're going to deliver and setting expectations along the way.

It was a culmination, really, of saying there's a good idea here. I even asked, "Am I the right person to execute that idea?" I asked my advisors and my early supporters, "It's a good idea and if I'm not the right person, let me find the one who is because it's a damn good idea." As I evaluated that, it just hit on all of my cylinders and I was personally excited about it because I knew how to build channel, I knew how to build product, I knew how to build a team and I wanted to lead this business.

I also knew how to raise money, so that was helpful! Because if you don't know how to raise money, you're in trouble in this business. I'm raising different money than I have ever raised before. I've been involved in venture-backed businesses my whole career and understand that side of it as well. It was a culmination but it was a gradual one because I had to be certain that I had a big market, a good idea, a receptive market and one I felt I could execute on. The team I gathered around me I had worked with before, and that reduces execution risk and of course venture loves that. It seems that the stars were aligned. Quite honestly, the other piece that was really inspiring to me was that I had people wanting to write me checks personally before I formed the company, just listening to the idea.

Dudley: That was a good sign.

Denise: I took in a convertible note close to a million dollars and I never spent of a dime of it until I had my seed round. I told the people who wanted to be writing those checks that it was very nice and social proof but I wasn't going to spend it because I knew it took a heck of a lot more money to establish a regulated entity like this. I just put that aside and raised the seed round and then converted that into the seed round. Those folks have seen the appreciation because we did two and a half times growth between our first year of lending and our second year of lending. In terms of our valuation, we've also tripled our valuation between the Seed and the A and more than doubled it in B. We're returning value and that is what we set out to do and it's been a great experience. We have thirty-seven people now and recently moved our office and are ready to take it to the next level this year.

Dudley: Why now? Could this opportunity have existed ten years ago?

Denise: In 2008, you know all the things that happened in bank regulation. When banks retreated and went upmarket above a million dollar loan size, now typically, five million dollars is where they want to be involved, that left the small business person adrift. Unless you have a lot of net worth in your community bank, you've been a businessperson before or you have a business that's been running for two or three years, it's tough to get a loan other than SBA. Particularly, our size loan averages $425,000 and goes up to two million today, and that is either an SBA, a process that can be death by a thousand paper cuts. Or you're using your own equity or you're more established and you're able to get a conventional loan from a bank. There really weren't a lot of alternatives for someone in between.

I think regulation's not going to roll back enough given the processes that have been put in place in banks and the infrastructure. We see banks partnering with us for that origination now rather than getting in the game to originate. They don't have verticalization. Banks are horizontal. For the most part they're trying to serve a horizontal set of needs, not a vertical market. They don't deeply understand a vertical market.

Dudley: When you started, did you have an MVP? Can you walk me through that MVP and first loan? I've read where you've talked about how you self-funded Apple Pie. Did that include the first loan?

Denise: No. We were in business funded by venture before the first loan because we had to, as you might imagine, go through a lot of significant regulatory and legal layers before we could even do the first loan. We also had to raise the debt capital to do the first loan. We were very fortunate to have a commitment prior to being live with our platform. There is a chicken and egg problem in supply demand businesses, How do you get borrowers before you have loan capital and how do you get loan capital before you have borrowers?

It's really interesting. You have to have franchisors to get borrowers; you have to have money to get franchisors and borrowers. It is a chicken and egg. The way we manage that is very much the way I've managed a lot of those evolutions in rolling out a product, and that is to go to the market to tell them my vision and get inaugural members who want to participate in that vision.

I signed twelve franchisors and said, "I don't have any money, but you're going to love it when I do. You're going to get priority treatment and allocation. If you'll bear with me and be an inaugural member and be ready when I'm ready, this will allow me to go to market and represent you to attract capital. You're going to need to be my references for why this is a good idea because there's going to need to be diligence with investors."

It worked. It wasn't simple, as I describe it, it sounds simple, but that took over a year and a half of building trust with brands, getting advisory board members inside those brands, an executive team to support me in building the product and helping define it. It's the best if you could define your product with your market, and that's what I did. I asked them to join me in creating a transformation in franchise finance. There was enough pain that people raised their hands and did that and gave me so much of their time to help design the financial product and platform.

Dudley: The underwriting approach—one of the things I think is compelling is you have the franchisor that is underwriting the franchisee. That works as a filter for you because they're not going to let a franchisee pass through that doesn't have certain qualifications. Can you talk about how you look at underwriting the franchisor and then eventually the franchisee?

Denise: There's a lot of data available. Now, a brand needs to give us more data. Because if you think about it, if a brand has been in existence—we'll just use an example—for ten years and they have 200 units across the country. Our question is: How many of those are still open? That opened five years ago, seven years ago, three years ago? We look at that as a proxy for how the loan is likely to perform. We also take historical small business administration data and we analyze that. We have a lot of other sources of data. Many are proprietary, meaning we've been the first mover in obtaining data that helps us in that underwriting. As I jokingly told Peter [Renton], I'd have to kill him to tell him how I do all of that.

Dudley: Or was it a joke? Dun dun dun!

Denise: Not really. It's really a proprietary model. We utilize that and then there's very traditional borrower underwriting that goes on in terms of net worth, liquid net worth, coverage ratios, to ensure that the loan is right-sized for getting to break even if it's a new unit. That's really important. Franchise businesses that are built from scratch in terms of the units in a particular geography have different unit economics and things can go wrong. You can have a longer construction period; you can have a slower marketing ramp. You have to have a loan size that's going to weather that from a working capital perspective. You need to know what that margin of error is.

It's very much a data-driven assessment because we have benchmarks. We have the best benchmarks you could ever imagine because those 200 units that were opened have a performance history.

Dudley: The other component of de-risking that I think is interesting—and I'm putting this in relation to some of the other small business lending—is the franchisor provides a process, provides marketing and training for the operators. Can you talk about that as a de-risking element for your loan?

Denise: There are three reasons a small business fails and three reasons that a franchise fails. It needs to be the right location. The demographics need to support the unit volume objective. Foot traffic is another way to think about it if it's a walkup business. The second is the operator. The ability for that operator to actually execute and run the business. That largely goes to the franchisor's model for who is a good candidate to run one of these, and their filter plus our filter. The third is the support system that exists for that business. In a franchise model, it's business-in-a-box or a blueprint for how to do it. That's training, as you were alluding to marketing. It's how they, a system with systems and suppliers to use, standardization, monitoring, all types of templates to run the business.

If it was just a small business without a franchise, that support system is whoever Joe Pizza Shop gets in their support network, so it's not business-in-a-box, tried and true. That's the reason someone will succeed or fail, is do they have the right support? If they're the right operator and they've got the right location, then it's a matter of following the blueprint. That's really the three most important things. Of course, the unit economics have to stand on their own. That's independent and really a baseline. If a franchisor has created a business that franchisees can make money running, that's great. If they've got a low margin business and it's tough to break even, franchisees won't be as happy and could results in a higher failure rate.

Dudley: I understand your average borrower has a median net worth of $2m and a credit score greater than 750. Perhaps they pay at a little bit higher of a rate than what a traditional bank would charge. Why does that make sense for them?

Denise: Couple of reasons. One is simply time and ease. If they've been through an SBA loan before, they can often look at that as a daunting process. Also, when you have a landlord's market, you need to commit to a space in a timely fashion and the landlord requires that you have proof of your loan approval. You don't get to sign the lease without demonstrating that you can afford it. It's timing. It's the process itself and whether it's painful versus not painful. Also, if you're an owner that plans to open more than one unit, when you get an SBA loan over $300k, you have to commit all of your personal collateral. You have to commit your house and all of your assets. Lots of people don't want to do that. In our loan there's a personal guarantee but you don't have to commit your personal real estate or other assets. It's just a different mindset in terms of comfort that you can build your business and your home is not part of the equation.

I think the other factor is—and this is going to be more true this year than in past years—SBA loans, in many cases, are variable interest rate loans. When you look at what your payment might be if it went up one point and you evaluate our loan compared to that, you're going to make a trade off. You're going to say, "It's just like a mortgage. I'm more comfortable in a fixed for seven years than a variable rate."

Dudley: What are the terms for the companies? What type of rate range are they borrowing and then what are the returns for the investor?

Denise: Our book right now is returning about 8.6%. We have a published range of eight to 12%. I think our highest loan was 12%, but the majority of them, because we underwrite such high quality borrowers and brands, are between eight and 10%. Rates are going down currently.

Dudley: Then the length?

Denise: We've got three different products. We have five year with seven-year amortization, a straight seven year, and we have a seven-year with ten-year amortization.

Dudley: How has the performance been so far across all your loans?

Denise: Great. Yeah, we're up over 120 loans, we put $65 million out the door. On an annualized basis, we have a 1.1% annual loan default rate and 0.7% annual net dollar loss rate.

Dudley: When a loan defaults and you foreclose on it, what
             does the collection look like? What assets are there
             to cover the principal of the loan? Is the franchise
             license a liquid asset?

Denise: The requirements in the loan are a personal
             guarantee, UCC filings on the business stuff, that
             there's a life insurance policy of course in the event
             of death that covers the size of the loan. A situation
             like that there's several steps that we take. One is
             we go back to the franchisors. Is there another
             franchisee—if it's not a location problem—that can
             assume that unit and buy it? That's a great outcome.
             Your recovery there is high, if the unit's performing
             and it's simply an operator issue that you can solve.
             The brand has the right if the unit's not performing
             to force the sale. There's a safety net there.

             If it's the operator's choice and they have some
             extenuating circumstance and they need to sell,
             there's a whole network of franchisees and we
             partner with people on resale. The brand is the first
             place to go for that but there's also a large business
             resale network out there that you can tap into. If it
             is a liquidation, and they need to sell the assets, we
             have the right to take the assets and sell them. There
             are many, many paths there. I won't describe all of
             them, but the risk mitigation is that the franchisor
             can get involved. The landlord will typically give
             some rent relief. The franchisor will give royalty
             payment relief, train the new operator at no charge
             and they'll do all kinds of things to help change
             the economics temporarily so that a business can

get right sided if it's just a matter of putting a new operator in.

You don't have that situation so much with an average small business on the corner. You don't have a place to go. There's no resource for that other than a brokerage network for resale, and it's tough. I think the fact that we have the franchisor and there are many things the franchisor can do is a major plus. They can contact the landlord on our behalf and work out an adjustment. The Franchisor has typically dealt with a landlord in some geography's more than one time and they help their franchisees negotiate those leases so it's a natural conversation for them to have. There's a lot of relationship and a lot of what I call teamwork in the recovery process.

Dudley: Do you see banks as a partnership model as opposed to an acquisition?

Denise: I do. You mean ultimately them acquiring a company like ours?

Dudley: Yes.

Denise: I think that's an option, but if you think about the amount of money that you need over time, you have to look at whether that single bank really is able to do that and doesn't constrain your growth. There are a few regional banks that are rising to that kind of size. That's what hurts a lot of the lending platforms, being too limited in their capital sources. You certainly aren't going to walk up to the altar with one of them because when you're operating as an independent you need to know that you have multiple sources of capital because of the constraints and definitions around diversification and concentration. If I have a brand that's growing really fast and I want to write a lot of loans for that brand, I'm going to need more than one source of capital to do that effectively today. It's a balancing act.

At the end of the day, when all things are proven out, can a bank have less concentration requirements? That's what's going to answer the question because it would be a limiter for our growth if they couldn't.

Dudley: There's an often-repeated phrase or statement that Millennials would rather go to a dentist than a bank. Do you believe that's true, and how does that tie in with the conversation?

Denise: It's interesting. The franchise industry has a Millennial kind of segment that it's developed and nurtured, more through education. It's called "Next Generation," because what you're going to see is Millennials taking over family businesses like this where the parents are either going to back them because this is a gig economy right now for young folks, and eventually if their parents do own something they're going to pass it on as an option if there's interest, just like a family-run business. Millennials will begin to represent ownership in this space. I don't see it a lot yet. I'm actually seeing not only Millennials but thirty-somethings being personally guaranteed by their parents to own a franchise.

You'll start to see that. That's going to be an emerging segment I think over the next ten years. Today, we serve three different kinds of borrowers. Ours are going to skew in their 30s and 40s and 50s. You don't see people in the retirement age so much getting in on the ground floor of a franchise, but you will see these up and comers. From a banking perspective, they're going to walk in with different expectations. Even those that are working in those businesses as managers or running or operating something on behalf of the franchisee are going to drive those kinds of changes over time. The younger people are going to tell people you're doing something the old-fashioned way; you should be doing this.

Dudley: Isn't that the truth? Playing a little devil's advocate here: what's a situation where Apple Pie and the industry in general go bad? What's the risk here? What keeps you up at night or concerns you?

Denise: I sleep really well, Dudley.

No, I've learned to sleep well in spite of whatever I carry around with me during the day. It's kind of essential to well-being.

Look. I was told once, Ron Suber's a good friend of mine and he said, "Denise, you're always going to have one side of the market or the other lopsided. You're either going to have too much demand and not enough capital or too much capital and not enough demand."

I've lived a bit of a charmed experience in that because I've had just-in-time money and I've always had more demand than I could fulfill. I haven't yet hit—I mean I've certainly gotten close because raising money in this last iteration was difficult as you might imagine for reasons that we won't necessarily spend time on here—but the industry suffered a little bit this year [2016]. That didn't make it easy for some of us, but I will also say that it actually helped some of us because the fact is people got spooked about the space but then they recognized differences in the models because they had to look further and deeper.

I got a lot more attention when that happened because people thought, "Hm, here's a business that has very low origination costs, had no delinquencies, no defaults,"—this is the last two years—"and they did what they said they were going to do and they grew. Better take a closer look because we're not liking the yields we're seeing on the paper we've bought and maybe this is the right asset to own."

I think it's always about the balance between capital and demand on the origination side. We have not experienced that acutely yet. I think the big question for businesses like mine is: where is the evergreen source of capital that is the best capital? We've gone through the analysis around recession or changes that could occur and if you look at franchise, yeah, fewer units opened in some sectors during recession, but if you think about the everyday services, people still eat out. In fact they downgrade their meals and therefore quick service restaurants do better in recession. Do people stop getting haircuts? No. You might get them at eight weeks instead of six but you still get them.

Revenues change and franchisors are resilient. They've lived through these times. They know what to do. They change their royalty, they give them royalty holidays, they do all kinds of things to deal with the economic changes that occur in order to do well during and through those times. We feel like we have a lot of layers of protection around some of those concerns. Look, if you have to grow slower, you grow slower, but this is a business. Lending to franchises has been around for decades and it's a solid industry that keeps on marching and growing. We feel it would be a matter of capital. Bringing the right capital to the table is always going to be the most important thing for us. I think if we can do that, the game's really over from an origination perspective because nobody wants to spend time looking for money. Nobody.

Dudley: Yeah!

Denise: I don't and they don't.

Dudley: Speaking of raising money, you recently signed a $180 million loan purchasing agreement. Can you talk about how that's going to change your business in the next couple years? Then also on the equity side, you raised equity from a well-known bank (Fifth Third) and a very well-known VC shop (QED) that were your co-leads. Can you talk about how—and in particular the VC has done multiple rounds with you—how those relationships are important in your growth?

Denise: On the loan purchase agreement, that's a great opportunity for us. It's over the next two years. That's the most capital we've ever had. It's triple what we've put out to date so it gives us growth. Also, for the first time there's a bank partner involved in providing leverage into that fund— it's a fund with $60 million in equity coming from a private equity firm and the balance coming from a bank as a leverage partner to them. We actually worked with the bank and put the two firms together. We know the bank has been active in the space and worked with another platform directly—GreenSky—we think we have a lot of parallels with GreenSky that the bank liked which made it easier because they have previously worked with a platform like ours and that created a blueprint for the next platform. The bank feels our model will stand the test of time and are investing on that basis.

I think that's a good proof point for us for the next round of capital on the debt side. We have two more loan buyers interested. Colchis was in our equity round and are interested in buying loans. We have another large undisclosed, due to privacy, buyer of loans. I would say today we have three strategic loan buyers, not just one, and so we're really set on capital. We have a fourth and fifth at the door. Capital's not currently the constraint.

On the equity round, that was an oversubscribed round. I'll say first and foremost, QED is the partner I think you're referring to. My other two equity investors who have been with me since the seed round were also in this round. Everybody bought into this round from the previous round. QED is extraordinarily strategic on the fintech side. I have so much resource available to me through QED. Really they bring a great amount of value in terms of benchmarking within their portfolio companies, providing guidance and sitting on our Credit Committee. They also hold an annual CEO summit of fintech CEOs that I attend. It is a two-day intensive where I get to learn from other CEO's. I've done my third one this past year and it's just been amazing.

I feel very fortunate because Frank Rotman and Nigel Morris have been at my side helping me build this business from the beginning. I couldn't ask for better partners. I think one unique thing about my venture firms is that all three of them started with their own money in their funds and one of them still, to this day, does not take outside LP (limited partner) money. That's a big statement for a venture firm.

I think because they were entrepreneurs and they were business builders, I got very lucky because all three of them contribute to my business in a real, practical and pragmatic way and we're very transparent with one another. I see them as business builders that are with me in good times and in bad. Fortunately, I haven't had a bad board meeting but I think if I did, I wouldn't call it a bad board meeting. If I had disappointing news I think that I would have partners at the table helping me.

I think that the banking partner who is in the equity round is one of the most innovative community banks I have ever come across. We spoke to probably thirty banks last year and probably a hundred Wall Street firms that ran funds that buy alternative assets. In that walk, you can imagine, you can start to compare and contrast. Of the banks that I spoke to—Fifth Third was the most buttoned down, fast, clear at assessing equity and clear at looking at strategy from the bank perspective and helping us see how we might work together. They're phenomenal partners. I just actually came back from Ohio Friday night visiting them and they are, bar none, the best bank at working with a firm of our stage. I've never seen a bank move like they do.

Dudley: That's certainly a compliment. I want to just make sure, I appreciate the clarification on the $180 million. The capital stack is $60 million in equity and then a bank is lending $120 million on that as part of it?

Denise: Yes, as part of the leverage.

Dudley: I think that's really interesting because if the bank, who's been a partner of yours and been involved in the business, is willing to give that sort of leverage, to me that is a lot of confidence and very supportive of the quality of the credit behind the loans.

Denise: Agreed, agreed.

Dudley: I didn't know that's what the stack looked like. That's fantastic.

Denise: I've been really amazed. One of the measures, I asked Frank Rotman at QED, "If you were going to measure me in the first year of the business, how should I think about that?"

He said, "When you start out a new entrepreneurial venture, you usually have lots of onions to peel. You've got five or six big issues to tackle. If you can get it down to one in the first year, you will be really, really successful."

I loved that measure because I did get ours down to one problem. It was capital the first year. Then we got that problem solved in year two, and then it becomes about growth and scaling. Then there are other measures. You have to look at how fast should you grow and what's responsible growth. I really look to my venture partners as a place to understand how to think about these things, because you can't concentrate on everything at the same time. You've got to pick your areas of focus and generate value and understand working backward, what's that going to look like? What do I have to do this year to return value to my investors? Even if you're not talking about a liquidation event, you're just talking about doubling or tripling your value, what does that look like? Does that foot with how fast you can grow?

Dudley: Is there an overarching message you want delivered? Is there something that you want people to know and understand?

Denise: I'll break that down into audiences because on the investor side and the people who will own these assets, there's a time and place for people to feel the risk reward is there for them and some people will sit on the sidelines and watch. Others will jump in earlier. It's the old saying: you've got your early adopters and your late adopters. I think right now, the greatest amount of wealth in this country is with family offices and high net worth individuals. That's where the wealth exists. The wealth channel that money into asset managers who take fees and ultimately purchase assets like ours. Or it's banks with depositors' money, and you've got your borders on that and restrictions and protections.

I think that there is something happening in this economy and you see it in equity financing now with the various regulation changes where people can have access to assets and make their own decisions and choices. I hope that we become more efficient as a capital market and capital society. I hope that people gain access. I didn't mention this but every loan that we put in our marketplace where high net worth can purchase a fractional share, those individuals fund about 25% of every loan that we make and I never marketed to high net worth actively. It was an organic growth from my network and people who knew one another and also from the franchise industry investing in these loans.

I think there's a lot of power here where you're cutting out the middleman and making your own investment decisions, but I think an asset has to mature before people are largely comfortable doing that. I'd like to see one day a more efficient way to match capital with need. There has to be a lot of safeguards and performance history and all of that to make that happen, but that would be an interesting world if that were to occur. Some family offices are very smart and have chief investment officers that can evaluate these assets, but it's a very fragmented space and it's not one you can really tap easily without concerted effort and expense.

I think on the franchise side, we're really in for the long game. We don't have all the right and best money today to serve all of the industry effectively, but we want to be a one-stop shop that really provides a growth engine for the franchise industry, for its operators. That would be in both debt and equity, and one reinforces the other. We want to be a holistic transformation agent in franchise finance and we want to make it easier, better for growth. I also love the fact that we can wake up every day and know that when we fund a franchise we just created jobs. That's just an added fun benefit for us.

Then I would say on the people side, I'm really excited about building the culture of our business.

Fifty percent of our people today have known somebody in the business prior to coming here and that helps us with culture because as you get further degrees of separation on that, it's harder. I just have a lot of intention around building a great culture and a great company that serves the franchise industry like it has never been served before.

Frank Rotman: Founding Partner, QED Investors

www.qedinvestors.com

QED IS INVESTING their private capital in fintech focused businesses. Some of their successes are extraordinary. QED was one of the earliest investors in SoFi, Prosper, Avant, Green Sky, Credit Karma and LendUp among many others. Most of these companies have reported private valuations greater than $1 billion. As an early investor, hitting on one would be extraordinary. Hitting on multiple is without description.

Frank and the QED team have an amazing background I am excited to include. Before QED, many of the founding team took a credit card spinoff out of a regional bank and built what is now known as Capital One. The team recognized in the mid-1980s that credit cards were about information and that the credit card industry might be at the forefront of the technology revolution.

In my opinion this team is unearthing opportunity just as they identified with Capital One. QED recently announced a partnership with Fifth Third Bancorp. QED will advise Fifth Third on fintech strategy that complements their internal innovation efforts.

Dudley: Would you explain the genesis of QED and the background of the founding team?

Frank: QED investors is a boutique venture capital fund that was formed nine years ago by three of us that had a shared work history, in that we were there in the early days of helping to create what became Capital One. Nigel Morris was the co-founder of Capital One. Caribou Honig is another founding partner of QED, and he spent ten years in a variety of roles at Capital One including leading its early foray into the Internet. I spent twelve-plus years there building businesses from scratch that the company needed, or fixing some of the big businesses when they were broken. I also spent a fair bit of time building out the risk analytics of the company, working with some of the big operational areas, and helping diversify the company into different asset classes and geographies.

We each left Capital One to pursue different opportunities, but joined back up nine years ago to form QED Investors, and since then we've been investing our own capital in typically early-stage companies. We're operators disguised as investors and our whole goal is to help smaller businesses turn themselves into bigger and healthier businesses that ultimately will stand the test of time.

In the past nine years we've grown the team and are now ten strong. There's quite a bit of Capital One DNA in our ranks which serves us well given the types of companies we're interested in helping.

Dudley: QED's founding team had the vision to see the opportunity with Capital One and now you have evolved in to a successful venture capital group with a focus on investing in fintech. What are you seeing that others do not?

Frank: We're not unique in our views of how the fintech ecosystem is evolving, but I do think that there's one prevalent trend that has influenced all of our investment decisions. At a high level, the theme is one of atomization or fragmentation of the value chain. For instance, in lending, there are capabilities and infrastructure that you need in order to make a loan. The fragmentation of the value chain has made it such that you can assemble your own business model around a competitive advantage and find third parties to plug the gaps. As an example, you could be a specialty originator with expertise around finding customers and putting them through an incredibly friendly user experience that's frictionless. In this model, you should be able to connect with lenders on the back end who are willing to define a credit box they're comfortable with and then buy the loan production as it comes through your system. Or, if you wanted to be a lender, you could partner with a bank like a Web Bank or Cross-River Bank to create, manage and monitor the program while owning the majority of the loan production on the back end. You can assemble the model any way you want and don't need to be all things to all people. You don't need all of the capabilities in-house because there's a way of buying the things that you don't have or renting them from the general market.

Dudley: Doing my research on Capital One, there was a saying that was used a lot—credit cards are just data. Do you see this very similarly to lending platforms, and is there more data today, and is more data always a good thing?

Frank: I think Capital One evolved over time. In the very early days of Capital One—and it's sad to hear myself repeat this—but we thought of consumers as packets of NPV (Net Present Value). This narrow view served the company well for a number of years and helped establish the solid analytical frameworks that Capital One is known for even today. Making sure that we had the right product for the right customer at the right time based on all the information we had at our fingertips was what Capital One was all about. Over time Capital One evolved and realized that there's a lot more to building a franchise than thinking about customers as packets of NPV. Consumers made their buying decisions about products in a lot of different ways and on a lot of different dimensions, not all of which were easy to describe using raw data. Building up true marketing, consumer and servicing DNA took time.

Fast forward to today and Capital One has evolved into a full-service banking organization that cares about the customer. I think it started with data and evolved into a lot more over time. I think that the marketplace lenders and the next-gen specialty originators that are out there today are starting with an area of focus and building the business on that particular pillar. Each one has its own value proposition, but the common thread is that they're starting with fixing user experience issues, most of them during the application process or the onboarding process, and a lot of them then continue that user experience into servicing. Today's innovation is grounded in the recognition that customers want frictionless products. They want to apply for and use them on the devices that they care about. They don't want full form applications. They want information pre-filled. They want to be able to buy something with clicks of buttons rather than uploading lots of documentation and going through a high-friction exam.

Most of the next-gen players in fintech are starting with the user in mind and are experts on product design, user experience, interfaces and APIs. Marrying these capabilities with a deep understanding of the complexities of the product itself isn't easy. In lending, you need to understand approve/decline, pricing and credit extension decisions; and if I'm honest, it's a lot of hard work to manage products that at their core are complex annuities. And lending isn't the only corner of fintech that's experiencing a lot of change. Small business customers need invoicing solutions. Money is being moved across borders by consumers wanting to get money to family members back home. And consumers want to conduct most of their core banking in-app vs. in-branch. In all of these corners of the banking ecosystem the next-gen players are starting with a better user interface and user experience and then pairing it with the right product.

Dudley: Is marketplace lending, and fintech more broadly, an iteration on the banking model? Or is this an inflection point in the business altogether? And if it is an inflection point, is there historical precedent?

Frank: There are a lot of ways at succeeding in giant markets, but when you stare at banking, there are a handful of distinct profit pools, and every single one of them is under attack. It doesn't mean that the fintechs are going to completely wipe out banking the way it exists today. In fact, I don't believe that. I'm much more of a centrist because I believe that the banks are very good at a lot of things. They're very good at understanding the financials of the annuities that they're creating. They're very good at protecting the deposits of their customer base and somewhat good at figuring out from an asset allocation standpoint how to deploy them. They're good at ticking and tying everything together from a process standpoint so that mistakes are minimal. And they're very good from a regulatory standpoint to make sure that everything they do is done in a compliant manner.

So, while banks are very good at a lot of things, fintechs typically are better at the tech component of the business which results in better user experiences. They're better at understanding down to the customer of one what the customer wants.

They're better at defining unmet needs and building solutions around these underserved customers.

There really are benefits that each side has so the real question is: In the future are the fintechs going to evolve and look more like banks or are the banks going to evolve and look more like fintechs? I think on the banking side you have to ask how good they are at partnering. How good are they at shipping code? My view is that they're getting better at partnering but that they're actually pretty terrible at shipping code because they're building it on top of very archaic code bases that are just hard to manage. It's not that the people aren't smart or talented within the banks. It's not that they don't have good ideas. It's a legacy issue and not one that's easy to solve. They're building off of code bases that are really hard to manipulate. The fintechs absolutely have an advantage on shipping code which is really paramount to what it takes to innovate.

On the fintech side of the ecosystem, it's acutely clear that they aren't as good at some of the things the banks are good at. They don't have access to the customer bases the banks do. They don't have access to deposits the same way that banks do. They don't have the experience in working with regulators and dealing with the compliance environment that we're in the same way that the banks do. You almost have to ask yourself, "Who evolves in which direction?" because I think the light fintechs have to get heavier, and the heavy banks have to get lighter.

Dudley: Build, buy, partner, or be bought. Can you expand on this, and in particular SoFi's recent acquisition, and how you see this evolving?

Frank: I'm going to stay away from commenting about any particular company, but I would say in general, as the fintechs evolve and start proving out that they have a value proposition that customers want, it's very natural for them to expand their offerings into other products and services. This is especially true if they're serving a very distinct slice of either the consumer or the small business universe. In the case of a company going after a particular demographic, or lifestyle, or stage customer, it's very natural for them as they build out one product to think about what other products they can offer their franchise.

            I think you're going to see some of the successful fintechs add more products to their mix, or if they have one particular product that they're exceptionally good at, start to offer it through as many channels and geographies as they can. Again, there's no one answer here, but I do think that you're going to see an evolution both in terms of how the fintechs have to expand as well as how the banks have to evolve their products into ones that are much more modern and served up through channels and interfaces that consumers want.

Dudley: Any coincidence to the growth in fintech coming out of the Great Recession?

Frank: It's a good question that I'm not sure I have any answer to. Innovation does come in waves so sometimes it's difficult to understand causality. When it comes to fintech, I think that coming out of the recession the banks were on their heels fighting a rear-guard action. They were spending a lot of time and effort improving their capital ratios as a reaction to the emerging regulatory environment. The problems that they were facing were big and severe and if not addressed quickly could have turned into "extinction" events. The incumbents were fighting for their lives on critical dimensions which gave a little bit of breathing room for some of the next-gen companies to start to capture market share. It was a scary time, because it was difficult for the small, emerging innovative companies to attract capital during a period when everyone else was retreating or retrenching. It was a difficult environment to operate in, but from an innovation standpoint there was a lot of room because the incumbents weren't really paying attention to what the start-ups were doing.

A good example of this is how Prosper and Lending Club emerged at exactly the same time that the banks were shutting down their personal loans business units. The banks were shutting their personal loans product lines down based on their experiences during the crisis, but at the same time a new business model was being built by a few start-ups that had real merit. The reason why these models had so much space was because there was a gap in the marketplace due to the banks shutting down the product. And by "shut down" I mean it no longer existed in their suite of consumer products.

There's typically opportunity to try new things when the big guys aren't paying attention to innovation especially when they're fighting bigger battles. This is my simple explanation for why we've seen a lot of activity coming out of the recession.

Dudley: Yeah. I think that's a really good answer. We've observed in other industries where technology can create a "winner take most" market. At the same time you hear conversations within the banks about consolidation and some of the regulatory burden, and how at scale they try to combat it. In a combination between those two, do you think it will create a system that's more robust, or more sensitive to "too big to fail"?

Frank: While there are a few exceptions to this observation, when I look at the US banking environment, for national scale businesses they typically collapse over time to a cadre of five, six, or seven major players that each have significant market share. The US is a big country, so you're not seeing a lot of "winner take most." What you're seeing are five or six players that are all fairly dominant in the space. Name a product category, name an era within banking, and you're probably going to be staring at five or six players that are capturing most of the profit. In the credit card space, it's not difficult to name them today, and while it might have been a different five or six players twenty years ago, the dominance of a handful of players existed then as well. It's the same in auto. Mortgage is a bit more spread, but you still have some very dominant players at the top of the list. If you look at the big brokerage houses or the wealth management companies, it's similar.

In this environment, there are some interesting new players nipping at the heels of the banks, and the question is: Do they break in to become one of the top five or six players in their category? I don't think that one of these new players will just snap their fingers and unseat all of the top five or six players nor do I think the fintechs are going to run over the banks and take over all of the top spots. But I do think there are some real contenders out there the same way that Capital One in the early days wasn't a top five credit card player. It worked its way into that position in a market where there were four or five other innovators growing and capturing market share. Capital One is still around and doing well while some of the other innovators were purchased by banks, some collapsed through poor decision making, and some just never grew into "relevance" and fizzled out.

Dudley: I don't think we have the answer, but I'm just curious on thoughts of robust systems versus those that are more sensitive to stress, and if this is helping or potential concentration could hurt.

Frank: Yeah. There are a lot of very large banks, and at the same time, the fintechs are growing, but they're nowhere near the size of the top five banking entities in the country.

Dudley: Sure.

Frank: Time will tell ten years from now if companies like SoFi become a $100 billion market cap company. The potential is there, but there's a long path to get from A to B.

Dudley: In regards to QED, you have a very strong portfolio whether it be consumer lending, business lending or fintech. You just announced a partnership with Fifth Third. Can you talk about how you're looking to evolve, and potentially tie in your portfolio with players like Fifth Third, and the strategy, how you see it playing out?

Frank: There's no grandiose plan for QED that looks twenty years in the future and defines what we're going to evolve into. We started off as three people who worked together at Capital One, and we're now a team of ten with a lot of Capital One DNA which means we can do a lot more. We're really trying to help companies build themselves into enterprises that can stand the test of time. That's still our core mission. We're operators disguised as investors and we love helping companies.

            As for our relationship with Fifth Third, it came out of the realization that we were frequently acting as a translator in the marketplace. Many fintechs are interested in talking to banks because they think that they need a bank to offer their service or their product/service would be good to offer to the bank's customers. At the same time, we were hearing from banks that they didn't understand this fintech thing. They didn't have access to all of the interesting companies, and when they did, they didn't understand how they operated or sometimes even why their products were "better."

The interesting thing is we found QED becoming a connector. We speak bank, but we also speak fintech. Over the past handful of years, we figured out how valuable this position is. The hard part is you can't align yourself with the thousands of banks that are in the country and serve anyone well, so we figured understanding one bank and getting to know it really well was a good thing. Understanding how the bank's executives think, what their concerns are, what they're looking for, and trying to help them achieve their internal goals by connecting them to some of the really interesting players in the space that we have access to, seemed to be a win-win for the bank and for the fintech community.

We see ourselves right in the middle as connectors, because we speak the language of both parties.

Dudley: Your investment portfolio and success speaks to itself, but now that you have this partner, do you anticipate that changing your deal flow at all?

Frank: No.

Dudley: You are the best, so I imagine the deal flow you get is pretty strong, but I didn't know if there are different conversations in terms of the deal flow, that they see this as a potential tie-up for portfolio companies.

Frank: No. I mean, the goal is to do what we do well, which is find and help companies, and if there's an opportunity to make an introduction to Fifth Third, or to introduce Fifth Third to these companies, we're there to make it happen. But it doesn't fundamentally change who we are and the type of companies that we're interested in. Sure, it's a great benefit when we can make the connection because it makes sense, but it doesn't actually fundamentally change our business.

Dudley: How will regulation change the industry, and do you believe lending platforms are taking it seriously?

Frank: On the second piece, the lending platforms that don't take regulation seriously aren't going to succeed. It's not an option. You have to follow the law.

So, there's no choice here. It happens to be that there are a lot of regulations, and it happens to be that it takes a lot of internal work to make sure that you're compliant. There are a lot of people that have an interest in looking over your shoulder and making sure you do things right, so there's a realization emerging in the fintech community that critical competencies that you have to have to be successful are in the realms of compliance, regulatory affairs, and capital markets. I know there's a broad appreciation at this point and it's now a commonly held belief that there are areas you have to take seriously and invest in from the beginning. It's not an option to just layer them on later. You have to do them well from the very start.

These areas have become yet another barrier to entry. The net result of having to worry about them from day one is that there's a very large burden that many small, very early stage companies need to take on.

In terms of the regulatory environment we're in, it's an environment shaped by the crisis that's very protective of consumers. It should be. Let's be honest: Ten years ago there were companies offering products that were out of control on many dimensions, and we can point to the mortgage industry as a poster child for the previous era. But usually when problems get big enough, the regulators come in and create a new environment for doing business that tends to put more controls and disclosure in place. For instance, we saw complaints increasing in the credit card industry and once the regulators were done the industry had new regulations to adhere to like the Card Act. It held the banks to a completely new standard of how to manage their credit card programs and laid out strict rules for various policies and transparency around disclosures. While painful to the banking community, I think regulation like this can be very, very good. It's healthy.

But, at some point the burden is so high that it can actually stifle innovation and actually prevent companies from doing the right things for the customer. The paranoia and the belts and suspenders that you need to put in place to make sure that you're compliant sometimes can cross over a line where you're paralyzed and shut down from doing new things. That's what we have to protect against. I absolutely believe that regulation is a good thing. Protecting customers is a good thing. Making sure that companies are compliant with the laws that have been put in place is a good thing. But at some point, there becomes a paranoia of trying new things that's unhealthy.

I know that's a strange answer, but hopefully it makes sense.

Dudley: No. The last part was actually a follow-up question I was going to ask, in terms of risk to protecting the incumbents who are using regulation as that, and how it needs to be avoided, at the same time, making sure that you check the boxes in terms of having regulations in place.

Frank: What's funny is that all the regulation is actually creating an opportunity for the fintech community to participate and help the banks. Regtech is a whole class of new startup that's emerging to help reduce the burden of the weight of regulation through technology and tools. Regulatory technology trying to help the banks become more efficient is a real thing and a great new trend to watch.

So when you peel apart the cost of this regulatory environment, you see that there's a large burden that's been put on every financial institution that's being solved by throwing human beings at problems that over time technology can help with. The policies created by the regulators could be the right policies, but to actually follow them requires a lot of human beings and adds a lot of cost to the system. If you look at CitiBank and Credit Suisse and Chase, between 10% and 15% of their global workforce is working on compliance matters. This equates to tens of thousands of human beings doing things that machines might be equally good at, if not better. At the very least a huge percentage of the work that's being done by people could be done all by machines and algorithms which in turn will allow the people in the system to concentrate their efforts in more needed places. AML (Anti-Money Laundering) and KYC (Know Your Customer) are two big areas where there's innovation taking place in the fintech community, and I think it's incredibly healthy and helpful to the banking community.

Dudley:　Your background at Capital One, in terms of credit underwriting, was pretty extensive, and now as you have your investor hat on, it's a unique profile. What are your thoughts on the underwriting quality on the platforms generally and how has that evolved, and how do you see it evolving? I talk to VC folks in the space, and I see some lacking in terms of what I would perceive as due diligence on the underwriting platforms, and then I've talked to credit folks, and they don't necessarily see the opportunity here, and they focus all on the underwriting. You have a good balance of both, I would say, and so I'm interested in this perspective.

Frank:　Underwriting matters. It's not like it's a topic that can be ignored if you're backing a lending company. Lending is a very easy thing to grasp conceptually but it's incredibly difficult to manage well. You're handing someone cash today for whatever need that they have and you're trading it for a stream of cash flows in the future that has variability and volatility associated with it. Structuring and managing a complex annuity is really what lending is all about. You have to understand when to approve or decline an applicant, understand pricing and how it affects positive or adverse selection, understand how much credit you can make safely available to an individual, understand what collateral you need and what that collateral is worth, understand how to look at the identity of the individual, their ability to pay, their willingness to pay, the stability of their income, etc. Every single one of these dimensions is important when it comes to managing the annuity.

What I will say is that some of the more sophisticated banks are really good at this. From a credit standpoint, I know personally the quality of the work and analysis being done at places like Capital One and it's incredible. It doesn't mean that this is true throughout the entire banking community, but the best banks can hire the best talent, and are really good at the analytics that drive the profitability of their business lines. Where the fintechs are good from an underwriting standpoint is that they're adopting newer techniques faster with machine learning being a good example. They're willing to experiment with new data sources and try things out that some of the big banks are a little bit scared of because of compliance and regulatory concerns.

The newer players need to be cognizant that they too have to care about Fair Lending and other important regulations that affect approve, decline and pricing decision. They can't use any data source however they want, so there's a lot of learning in the fintech community about how the rules actually need to be applied and practiced. I also think that machine learning can be fantastic, but it's just a technique and is really just an input to a more comprehensive credit policy. The machine learning algorithm might be good at taking historical data and pulling out as much signal as possible from it, but environments change and this can be problematic for machine learning techniques. Competitive environments and economic environments change, and change affects what an annuity is going to look like and how it's going to perform. Credit policy analysts have to think about the fact that models are only trained on what they've seen and that credit comes in cycles that can't be ignored. If the data isn't being trained on the right cycle or the next cycle looks different than the previous cycle, then the models are blind and need help.

You have to marry the best of data analytic techniques like machine learning with good, solid underwriting, and good, solid belts-and-suspenders policies that aim to produce annuities that perform both in good and bad times. The real goal of a solid annuity is to be great when times are good but not so bad when times are bad. It's important to reduce the volatility through cycles if you're going to build a healthy loan portfolio.

Dudley: What concerns you that's a risk to the growth of fintech?

Frank: There's a lot of capital that's flowed into the ecosystem, and that means that many new companies have been formed and not all of them have a true reason for existence in the marketplace. You have to be careful when there's a lot of capital flowing into a space that players don't ruin a market irrationally. You have to worry about the fact that if there are a lot of players, there's confusion for where the next dollar of capital should go because it's not always obvious who's winning. Just dealing with such a vibrant ecosystem is problematic until it flushes itself out. But, just to be clear, within this community of new startups there are some amazing businesses that are being built. It's just a difficult exercise trying to figure out which ones should be backed and how they stand out from the rest. Time will solve this issue.

Dudley: It always does, right?

Frank: It should. Good companies perform well and continue to grow, and ultimately the economics tell the tale. The mediocre and bad companies will have problems attracting capital over time, but right now, there's still a lot of capital flowing into the space. Over the last twelve months it's slowed down a bit which is actually very healthy. The way I like to think about building these businesses, you typically have to revenue your way into a good business and then when you hit scale you cost your way into good margins. Growth is life. You have to prove that you can build a product and attract users such that you have a reason for existing in the ecosystem. Over time a company works its way into scale economics and I think a lot of the recent startups are going through the phase where they've proven they can grow; now they have to do the hard work of delivering good margins. This is my view of the next stage in the evolution of the space.

Nathan Popkins: Founder, Align Income Share Funding

www.helloalign.com

[Nathan tragically passed shortly before the publishing of this book. Please reference 'In Memory' at the beginning of this book.]

A LIGN INCOME SHARE Funding is taking a dramatically different approach to consumer lending. Align is "aligning" itself to share in borrower success and challenges via an income share agreement. Align has raised over $31 million in institutional capital.

A skeptic will ask, "If this is such a good idea, then why is this only happening now?" To validate income requires a central clearinghouse. The IRS is effectively this clearinghouse. However, to validate at scale requires robust and inexpensive technology architecture.

The individual with low or tight liquidity draws a disproportional benefit from an income share agreement. With few cash reserves, a fluctuating income can cause challenges when trying to meet fixed debt service and living expenses. How big is this market? Recent reports suggest 50% of Americans have less than three months of living expenses on hand. That is a big addressable market.

Dudley: What is Align Income Share Funding?

Nathan: We are a consumer finance company. We provide funds to consumers in exchange for a percentage of their salary or wages for some predefined period of time. That structure is called an income share agreement, or sometimes you'll see it referred to in academia as a human capital contract. Sort of the idea behind that arrangement from the consumer's perspective, having sort of that equity-like structure, is a more flexible structure and one that should be more inherently affordable for the customer. As their income fluctuates—typically in scenarios where their income goes down—that's a scenario where their ability to meet their other monthly financial obligations is going to be increased as well. By lowering their payment's proportion, we help get them current. We help keep them from falling behind. The trade off in exchange for that, [for] folks who have their income go up or rise somewhat, the payments go up as well. It looks a bit more like making kind of an equity-style investment in this person instead of giving them a monolithic fixed-rate loan.

Dudley: When you talk about equity side relative to debt, what does that mean?

Nathan: Specifically, the product that income share agreements compete with, broadly speaking, would be any sort of traditional consumer loan, [which] over the longer term could range from mortgages, and credit cards, and auto loans. Specifically, when I talk about our company, the product that we compete with that we're trying to replace is what [are] known in the market as installment loans. Installment loans are typically loans where a consumer receives funding. In exchange for that funding, they make a fixed series of payments. Usually monthly payments [made] over a time period ranging from as short as a few months to as long as a few years. A lot of the folks who take out personal loans or installment loans fall into the segment of the consumer market that we would deem consumers with thin or minimal personal liquidity. The way we define that is an individual who has less than three months of living expenses available in cash, checking, or savings that they can draw on to meet their financial obligations.

Those folks derive a disproportional benefit from the income share product, because they are not meeting their monthly financial obligations from their balance sheet. From cash that they have on hand, they are meeting their monthly financial obligations: paying their rent, paying their phone bill, their water bill, and things like that they are paying those with income that they have coming in real time. Consequently, someone who is meeting their financial obligations with their income; if they see an adverse change in their income—if they get laid off, or they're disabled, or they've got some seasonality—that is going to make it harder for them to meet their financial obligations that month. Our product lowers the payments that they owe in those scenarios. Our product should be much more forgiving, much more inherently affordable, and allow them to stay current in those situations. That's who we are competing against.

Dudley: When you say competing, what existed in this space prior to the income share agreement? The option would be credit card, or installment lending. Do you envision this product replacing a significant amount of market share from those traditional lenders where you're targeting the same customer?

Nathan: That's correct. In fact, it's self-reported, but we track what our applicants or what our consumers say that they are using their funds for. The number one thing that they are using their funding for is to replace or refinance out of some other form of more traditional loan. That is usually credit cards or some other fixed installment loan they want to refinance out of and replace with our product instead.

Dudley: Are they refinancing out of that product because it's more costly? Or is it the concept of the income share agreement that they prefer? Is it easier for the customer to comprehend, in percent of income as opposed to APR?

Nathan: [It's] the combination of those things and it varies. Some of each. We may be a cheaper option for some folks. It's not obvious or not always true over the life of their contract; someone's monthly payments with Align wouldn't necessarily be lower than if they'd gone to a traditional installment lender and traditional installment loan. Sometimes we are, sometimes we aren't. The things you see though, people appreciate the insurance policy that comes into this. The inherent affordability, where they know, "Great, I'm employed today." I think—having come through, in the last decade, a generational low water mark from employment in this country—I think people appreciate the value of having some kind of employment insurance and disability insurance. Change in income insurance, baked into the product. People realize the value of that. Something that [only] takes a percentage of someone's income.

There's a number of studies on consumers and their understanding of various financial product, or terms that are in their financial products. People are, for example, notoriously bad at being able to calculate interest rate if you gave them a monthly payment, and principle amount, or vice versa. Those are terms that get lost from the consumer, and they generally find confusing and can't do the math on very frequently.

Conversely, pretty much everyone knows how much money they're making at a given time. That's something most consumers tend to be extremely focused on. We are taking a fixed, predefined, single-digit percentage of that amount. If I know that you're going to take 5% of my paycheck, I can look at my paycheck, multiply that by .05 [and] really easily and transparently figure out what I owe. In some cases, we may be cheaper, but I think that there's kind of that inherent affordability in a downside insurance. As well as good transparency, and some of the softer elements of the conceptual alignment of interest between us and the consumer. They make more money; they do better. If they make less money, they're worse off, but we're also sort of sharing that pain. Those are the elements; a sort of increment to our elements of our contract that exists in our relationships with our customers. They appreciate incremental instead of an installment loan.

Dudley: The mechanics of this: Someone agrees to borrow from you "N" dollars today. How does this work? What does the length of the term look like? What type of ranges are on the term? What type of ranges are on the actual percent of income?

Nathan: It expands over time; we may look to go into adjacent spaces to where we've operated historically. Our historical term, we have allowed contracts as long as six years, and as short as two years. We have generally provided consumers as much as $12,500 at a max. That's going to vary somewhat depending on some of the applicant's risk and income level and that sort of thing. We will take up to 10% of an individual's income; that's the max. The reality is, whenever a new applicant comes to us, we are giving them a specific offer that is specific to them and their income level and their employment. I think [on] the average we take about 5% of an individual's income. They can go up to as much as 10%; if they need a larger contract or something like that.

Dudley: I like examples. Let's say you and I had a contract and all was good for the first six months of the five-year deal. Then I lose my job. What happens to my payments? Let's assume that I get a job after four or five months of looking. Then what happens?

Nathan: In the scenario, you're out of work. Someone's giving out a percentage of their personal income. We define personal income narrowly. We only include a couple of things in that. We exclude a ton of things [that], for example, the IRS would tax, and the IRS would consider income that we don't consider income. Specifically, we are saying, "Your personal income is the fruit of your productive labor. Your salary, wages, tips, and commissions." Anything else falls outside of our agreement with the consumer. The consumer goes and gets an inheritance, wins the lottery, has some capital gain, has for example, unemployment benefits or disability benefits. When you go from earning a salary to now being unemployed, you may have some unemployment benefits coming in. Those are all things that the IRS will tax. We do not consider those personal income; we do not take a percentage of them. Those are immune from us taking a percentage of them.

From our perspective, your personal income just went from some positive number monthly, to basically zero dollars while you're unemployed and looking for work. It's worth taking, let's say, 5% of this individual's income. It's what they've indexed to us. 5% of $0 is $0. That customer will fulfill their obligations to Align while they're unemployed by making payments of $0 dollars to us in those months. While they make those payments of zero dollars to us, if they're unemployed, that counts as "paid as agreed" for their credit score. We are not extending the term of their contract. They don't go into a level negative amortization in their balance, or we're not increasing a balance or something like that. It is just contractually-forgiven payments. That's sort of part and parcel of the risk we're taking, while we're providing people with these contracts.

Five months later, after having gone five months without making payments, and they now find a new job [at] whatever that new salary or wage level is that they're at. We're now going to take our agreed upon percentage of that. If that's higher than what their salary was before they lost their job, then their payments will be slightly higher than they were five months earlier. If that new income level is lower, than those payments will be lower at a certain match with whatever that new income level is.

Dudley: How do you vet income? How do you know as a borrower, I am making what I say I'm making? It seems like there's a natural reason to undermine what you earn.

Nathan: There's a handful of ways. We do pretty thorough and rigorous income validation. It's going to vary from applicant to applicant depending on what they have available. We have a couple of third-party vendors that we use to validate income either through pay stubs or what's been reported to the IRS. We can look at what's being deposited via direct deposit into their account. We will frequently then cross-check that, or triangulate that to get

applicant-provided pay stubs, and/or one or two
years of tax filings with the IRS.

When we're using the IRS, for example, in our filings
to validate income, we have the applicants sign at
the outset of their contract. The agreements actually
allow us to go directly to the IRS to get those, as
opposed to getting them from the applicants. The
IRS is a pretty good collector, actually. It's hard for
them to defraud us without also defrauding the IRS.

Dudley: What you've developed is pretty intriguing. A
            lot different from what you see in the consumer
            finance space. Going back to Nathan: What's your
            background? How did you see this opportunity?
            What caused you to act on it? Why this and why
            not something else?

Nathan: Those are all related answers. Prior to this, I had
            been working in a couple of advisory firms, advising
            financial institutions on things like capital raising
            and mergers and that sort of thing. Specifically, a
            number of the companies that I worked with were
            in the consumer lending and specialty lending
            space. Within that, sort of a subset within that,
            were in the private student lending industry. That
            was actually how I became aware of the income
            share agreement product, through some folks
            who tried to use a similar product with students,
            either graduate students or undergrads, in [the]
            case of helping recent graduates refinance out of
            their private student loans. The product was very
            intriguing, very interesting. I was kind of curious as
            to why there hadn't been a broader proliferation of

this product, given the attractive features, alignment of interest, and inherent affordability of it.

Interestingly, I thought the student space was the very difficult one to focus on, at least from the perspective of building a company at the outset around it. It was one where I think due to a natural lag in cash flows, the once or twice a year funding cycle makes it difficult to innovate on the product, and iterate on it. With students, you have underwriting variables like GPA, and quality of [their] institution, and major, which all to varying degrees predicted future labor market outcomes. Not nearly as predictive as if I know what your income's been for the last several years; that can be highly predictive on what it will be for the next several years. I thought that student space is certainly a good use case of potential applications for the product. I thought it would be difficult to crack that egg appropriately up front. Instead, I did see though there was another market that I thought this product provided perhaps a more disproportionally positive alternative, relative to the other products that were in the market. That was that low liquidity consumer, who was looking for something that was kind of safer for them and more affordable than a traditional installment loan.

Really, part of what I think made me realize the potential opportunities [happened] around the time I was doing research initially on ISAs, and specifically on this market. There were some studies that were being done at the time that were sort of sizing the market. Frankly I was surprised how big it was. That statistic I used earlier, less than three months' worth of expense was available and liquid: cash, checking, savings. That appears to be about 50% of the adults in the US right now. That's the number that's actually increased over the prior generation. It comes from a background where a lot of my clients were more focused on higher income, or higher wealth customers. As I realized the size of this market (A), and the beneficial elements of this contract relative to the other products that were in the market (B), I became very interested, and in fact, that has been the market that we focused on as we founded the company.

Dudley: You did the research; you identified this is an opportunity. Then you just quit your job? What was the next step?

Nathan: Basically, I did a little bit more research. I wanted to make sure I really felt that there was a way to underwrite this risk in a kind of formulaic and automated way. I didn't want to be trying to decide what every applicant's future prospects where. I wanted to know if using these large data sets there's a way to build an algorithm or formula, to try to efficiently assess the risk in providing this product to new applicants. We're happy to report that after some research, we found what we felt was sufficient data to assess all of the risk in providing this kind of product to this population of consumers. Traditional credit risks, as well as the risk of non-payment due to things that are unique to this product like unemployment, or disability, or change in income risk.

I also wanted to make sure that I had a fairly clear path to figuring out how we would fund the product long-term. Through doing some research on that, we were able to find some more novel financial products that were in the consumer finance space that were either being securitized, or kind of had an active market among private investment funds and hedge funds. I was able to find that, get a decent idea of how we would find funding for this product longer term and at scale. Once I sort of checked those two boxes, I left my prior employer whom I'd been with for eight years. It's a great firm called Sandler O'Neil and Partners. Left Sandler; founded Align.

Initially, we were only self-funded. We did a pilot program of contracts that I basically just funded myself. The end game was six months to see how they performed. They performed well. Slightly exceeded what we had anticipated in our risk models. It was a small sample product that would actually go out and start to raise some money from investors. Which we did, and we have done a couple of rounds of investor funding since then, including our most recent round where we raised about $31 million in debt and equity capital from a number of private institutions. To help grow both the business as well as [to] expand on our portfolio.

Dudley: I'd like to go back to that first contract. You mentioned you funded out of your own pocket.

How'd you market it, what's the story with it, and how nervous were you that the model was going to work?

Nathan: Nervous, although I guess it was a small enough private program up front. If for whatever reason, [say] it totally didn't work, [I'd have said] okay, lesson learned and probably would've moved on, I guess.

We initially marketed the way I think a lot of new companies market. It's a great way to find new customers when you are a new company. It's not as great of a way when you're kind of a scale, but we just marketed through a [few] search engines: Google, Yahoo and Bing. Customers who were looking for some sort of financial need, either to refinance or consolidate other debts, or had some near-term bills that they needed to pay. They would see an ad online, in the jurisdictions where we operated, when they were doing their Google, Yahoo, or Bing searches. If they clicked on it, it took them to a really simple application page. Folks would submit the application; we would run them through our underwriting formula, and then get back to them and tell them, "Hey, it looks like you did (or you didn't) potentially qualify for an income share agreement." Then [we'd] work through the underwriting process with them. The very first one that we did was for $4,000 and the first one made me pretty nervous because the first one never made a single payment.

Dudley: Did you know that before making two?

Nathan: No, we did a group of about three in one week. That was right before year-end, and at the start of the subsequent year, we did another fifteen or eighteen over the course of a month. One didn't make his payment, but the majority of them did. In fact, even slightly more than our model anticipated. We were probably a little behind our model for the first month or two, given that the first one was a true first-pay default. Over the course of then six months between when we did that pilot program, and we did service these for the next six months, and on a cumulative basis, [we] slightly outperformed relative to what we anticipated for the portfolio.

Dudley: You quit your old job; you funded the agreements out of your pocket. The first one went bust, and you still kept going. Good to laugh about in hindsight. You keep talking about how you have aligned interests with the borrowers because you are participating on the income side. Presumably, the regulators would love you. Who regulates you, and how has your relationship been? What is the regulatory reaction to your product?

Nathan: It's been a fascinating thing. It's been a really interesting case study, actually. Innovation within financial services. This applies to other industries as well, but you have this extremely broad body of regulations that address consumer finance. They're prescriptive on what you can and can't do, but they're only prescriptive on the product that existed when the regulations were written. The putative regulators for Align would be the non-bank lending regulators; the set of regulators that oversee lending that is not done by banks, essentially. Those regulators are, by and large, not federal regulators. There are some federal regulations on non-bank lending. Then there are regulatory bodies at the state level, regulations at the state level that actually oversee this.

Any sort of non-bank lending, or consumer finance product, you don't have one regulator you're potentially dealing with. You have fifty, or maybe fifty-one I guess. We were very fortunate relatively early on in our life cycle to find really good regulatory counsel that's been able to help us navigate that. We sit here today before we go into any new state; we have a new proactive dialogue with the regulator in that state. It essentially plays out like this: "We've done all the research that we can on the regulations and existing case law in your state. Here is what we think our income share agreement will be in terms of what will be considered by your non-bank lending regulators. Is it a loan? Is it not a loan? What type of product is this and what are the relevant regulations and case law?" We sort of lead with that, but it's a dialogue. There's back and forth.

Of course, the regulator has an opportunity to come back to us and ask for additional information on the product. They have the ability to come back and tell us, "Yes, we agree." "No, we disagree." Prior to entering any new state, we will have sort of an affirmative step of being back from that regulator telling us their interpretation of the product, and the exact set of laws that we either are or aren't beholden to. That's it.

Dudley: As you look at this product and you look at where you are in the space, what is the addressable market? What do you think the opportunity is here?

Nathan: I think the element of this product that provides better outcomes for the consumer can be somewhat mitigated. You go to different parts of the consumer financing market, for example, an individual who has a lot of assets, regardless if they have a lot of income or not, may not derive a lot of benefits from an income share agreement. If they lose their job, let's say, they would still very easily be able to meet all their financial obligations just with cash they've got sitting around the house. Consequently, an income share agreement may not be much more attractive to them than a loan. Maybe they would just want a fixed-rate loan, instead of an ISA. That said, I think the alignment of interest and inherent affordability of the product are concepts that are applicable to the entire suite of consumer finance products. We focused where we did -- unsecured product with generally a near-prime consumer who needs a few thousand dollars looking for a couple year contract -- because that's where this product ([for] that sort of illiquid consumer) that sort of product provides the most relative benefit to the other products that are out there. Where we thought we had the greatest competitive advantage.

There's no reason that you couldn't structure a mortgage, or an auto loan, or something like a revolving credit product, like a credit card, that is also based on a percent of someone's income. All you need to do that is appropriate data on people and long-term labor market outcomes to be able to price that appropriately. I look forward ten, twenty, fifty years in the future: I think you could have student loans, which you are starting to see, mortgages, and all other sorts of products that are structured more like an ISA instead of a traditional loan.

People say, "If it's so great, why haven't we been doing it that way [forever]?" To sit down and negotiate a [traditional, non-ISA] debt instrument we need to come up with three terms: We need how much is the borrower going to get? What's their installment payment that they're going to pay back? What is the timeline for those payments? All three of those terms can be negotiated and known by both parties who are sitting at the table. We could've gotten together 3,000 years ago and had a loan based on that, right? With an ISA, it's kind of similar. How much money is the person going to get? What is the time frame for payback? But the other one, instead of being some sort of fixed payment stream, is a percentage of income.

To be able to make that work, you need the ability to verify someone's income. You need a central clearinghouse for that. Until we had the IRS essentially [as the] centralized clearinghouse that's validating everyone's income, it really costs to have this product like an ISA that's based on income.

The ISA provider fundamentally also has to be in an income validation business, which we are to a degree, but it would be much harder without the centralized system that everyone reports their income to. I would argue that even, I mean [we've] had an income tax in this country, for a little over 100 years now. The reason that you're still only starting to see these now [is because] you need some sort of relatively automated or real-time technology-enhanced way to be able to validate and check that income.

Really technology is what's been unlocking the ability to use ISA in consumer applications, where they didn't exist or were very difficult to use in the past.

Dudley: Just to review: You think the opportunity, why it's different today, is [due to] the IRS acting like a central clearinghouse? The marriage of that and the ability for you to automate the confirmation from that clearinghouse allows you to do this at scale.

Nathan: Exactly.

Dudley: Anything you would like to add?

Nathan: The only thing that comes up with some frequency that I think is important, and this is more specific to our product. In addition to the why now, or why this product, the tradeoff there is why not this product? Or what are the issues with it? I think the [reactions] are very misplaced, but you get people who have sort of a visceral, negative reaction to just the idea of the percentage of income. I've heard things as draconian as indentured servitude quoted back to me about ISAs, and fundamentally other people who are fighting the concept that maybe they have some misunderstandings [about what indentured servitude is]: Third parties making decisions on what your job could be for you. We're not telling anyone what their job can be [or] where they can go work.

We're not changing your decision-making ability whatsoever; we're just saying we're going to share the upside or downside based on what that is. I think [that's] the visceral reaction to either that or the idea of the percentage income. I would tell people, "Everything you've ever purchased in your entire life took a percentage of your income. The difference is the cup of coffee I bought coming into work took a different percentage of my income than it did the guy behind me." We think this is a more equitable way of structuring this. The idea that we're fixing this on the percent of income should not be a novel or threatening concept to people.

People get concerned about on the upside: "Couldn't I wind up paying you a lot more?" Then I would tell people, "You could, potentially." We give them right to buyout. That buyout calculation is fixed. We don't move up the amount it takes to buy us out if your income goes up. You can always buy us out for less than the initial amount of money we gave you after you've made your first month's payment. Which, folks would get worried about paying,

"What happens if my income doubled or tripled or something, and now I'm paying an exorbitant amount?" We don't see incomes doubling and tripling in our portfolio very often, if ever. To the extent that you do, those folks have a right to come back to buy us out and limit their total payments or exposure to us, if you want. But if your income goes up by $10,000 per year, and you're giving us 4% of your income, you still keep the remaining $9,600. People ONLY wind up paying us more when they're also better off. If your payments to us increased, then that means your income went up and you're keeping the vast majority of that, so you're still better off. Even though you're paying us more.

Jorge Sun:
Founder, LendingFront

www.lendingfront.com

J ORGE WAS ONE of the founding members of OnDeck Capital and served as its Chief Credit Officer. Alternative lenders are stealing market share and big banks are spending big dollars to protect theirs. LendingFront's tool is helping level the playing field. Jorge created a solution for banks caught in the middle to scale an online origination channel without significant tech development from a bank.

You will not be surprised to know Jorge believes small business lending is broken. Simply, it is not profitable for a bank to lend to a small business seeking $50,000 or $100,000. Yet this is most of the small business loan demand.

Jorge wondered how a market this big could be broken. He asked how he could enable incumbents (banks) to gain access to better technology and open lending to such an important component of US GDP. LendingFront is Jorge's answer.

Dudley: What is LendingFront and what is it solving for?

Jorge: LendingFront is a cloud-based platform designed
            for banks so they can lend to small businesses
            more efficiently. Currently, there are two methods
            that allow you to lend at scale. One is using the
            consumer method, which looks at the consumer
            bureau to assess business risk, which is entirely too
            simplistic.

            Or the commercial method which relies heavily
            on GAAP Financials, which is really designed
            for larger, more stable institution. This method is
            effective in assessing risks, but it's time-consuming,
            cumbersome and expensive. Given most small
            business loans are under 100K, this makes them
            unprofitable for a bank to originate.

            Small businesses represent about fifty percent of the
            GDP in the US but only represent a quarter of all
            commercial loans, meaning that small businesses
            are half as likely to get a loan, so there's a massive
            gap in the market. The reason is that small business
            lending requires specialized technology and data,
            and using consumer or commercial methods just
            does not work.

Dudley: How do you define small business?

Jorge: Small businesses are institutions, usually less than
            10 million dollars of revenue.

Dudley: You'd mentioned banks, your primary customer. Is
            there a certain size of bank that you work better with
            than others? What's different than what they have

now? What I heard from you is a lack of lending that's going into the space overall, so the answer to that question may be they're not really going after it now as aggressively as they could be.

Jorge: Well, in order for you to originate loans, you need to have the right technology. Our infrastructure allows you to source loans and manage them effectively. Our target market is banks between 200 million to about 10 billion in size. These size banks don't have the technology budget to build or modify their own platforms.

For these banks, most lending is done by a commercially trained banker. So lending is mostly manual and bespoke. We enable banks to take their small loan requests and add automation and standardization while letting the applicants do most of the work. This makes small loans more efficient to originate.

What we're basically saying to the banks is, "Bankers are expensive. Let them deal with the much larger, complex loans. Smaller loans can be self-served and automated."

Dudley: What type of loan volume have you processed so far and how long have you been doing it?

Jorge: We've been in business about two years. Our clients are processing over two thousand apps a month. We are on track to do over 20 million this year. Again, we're subject to how aggressive our customers are. As we find more customers, that volume will go up.

Dudley: The sales cycle has to be long with your target customer, so two thousand apps a month after only twenty-four months in operation is impressive.

Jorge: Again, we don't think of it that way because that is really coming from our clients. It's how aggressive our clients are.

Dudley: Can you walk me through your process with the underwriting, the funding, the lifecycle monitoring, any event triggers, and collections?

Jorge: We provide a customer portal to allow customers to submit all documents needed for underwriting. The system automatically pulls all third-party data such as personal credit; that information is presented to the underwriter, decision is made, offers are sent via the portal. The customer can e-sign the loan agreement and submit any closing documentation required. Once it's all received and verified, the system will fund the loan and act as the system of record.

Dudley: In terms of the underwriting and red-light/green-light, are there minimum thresholds that the lender uploads into the system and if a loan meets those thresholds and the bank okays it, it can automatically go to the bank's client and say, "You're approved for x?" Or does there need to be that human checkpoint at that part of the process or both?

Jorge: That's really up to the bank. We can automate the whole decision or allow for an underwriter to always review.

Dudley: In terms of the banks when they're inputting
           their thresholds, risk tolerance, lending goals and
           coverage ratios, how is it tailored for them? What
           does it look like from their side?

Jorge: We can code their credit policy and execute it at
           the loan level. What they see is the recommended
           action based on their credit policy, e.g. approval,
           decline, loan amount, terms, etc.

Dudley: How are you monitoring for fraud? How do you
           look at that in the system and guard against that?

Jorge: We enable banks to triangulate the information
           from many different sources such as credit bureau,
           bank account, social.

Dudley: Can you share a little more about how you're
           looking at social? I think the triangulating makes
           sense. The social component is interesting.

Jorge: Social data to us [is] free web-available data such
           as Google Places that has relevant small business
           value. In the case of Google Places, it can help us
           map the business and verify that it exists. Also, we
           can get a feel for what others are saying about the
           business which can give insights into how stable it
           is.

Dudley: Is someone compiling it by hand? It seems like the
           data that you're collecting is fairly robust. Can you
           speak to the extent that your clients are making
           these types of loans now, to what data they currently
           have versus what you're able to provide them? And
           the differences?

Jorge: A lot of the information that we're talking about is gathered by many of our clients. It's how they gather, put it together, connect and store it that's the problem.

           Manually collecting PDFs, tax statements and searching online for the business is slow and time consuming. We enable them to collect most of it digitally in one central location. The best data we can provide them with is the small business' operating cash flow information. This is something most banks still do not heavily use.

Dudley: You have a lot of information from the client's client and the client yourself. How are you looking at security and making sure there's not any risk?

Jorge: Standard procedures. Encryption. Firewalls. It's not our data. It's our customer's data. Again, think of us as just the technology. We're not holding a lot of that information. We're just enabling.

Dudley: Going a little bit into your background, there's a lot here. There's a lot of industry knowledge. There's a lot of technical knowledge required to build this. Can you talk about your background with OnDeck and your inspiration for the idea and your decision to launch?

Jorge: Sure. I'm a banker by trade. So I have significant lending experience.

           OnDeck was an experiment on three things. One, can we build the technology to lend differently? Can we build the right credit policy and profile using different information to get our money back? Third, do customers want the online originated loan product?

LendingFront's a natural outcome of my OnDeck and banking experience. It's a platform that gives banks the technology to lend to small business more efficiently, profitably leveraging what we learned previously.

Dudley: Why was this not a fit with OnDeck?

Jorge: At the beginning?

Dudley: The time you left.

Jorge: The way you want to think about it is: Was the market ready for this type of technology? The answer was no. We tried to do this early on and say, "Hey. Use our tech to lend differently." Bankers are risk averse. Banks tend to think they know everything. The answer was, "This sounds great, but we don't believe you. Why don't you go lend on your own and if it works, then fine." Guess what happened?

Dudley: That makes sense.

Jorge: You pivot. You become a lender yourself and you're like, "Holy crap. I'm actually really good at it," and then you're no longer an SaaS (software as a service) company. You're your own lender.

Dudley: Yeah. I guess I didn't put that together until you said that, but everything you said sounds like every conversation I've had with a banker. So that makes total sense.

Jorge: Bankers are incredibly set in their ways but I am starting to see a fundamental change in attitude towards technology. So, conversations are different now.

Dudley: With that in mind, what are one or two of the biggest misconceptions about your business?

Jorge: One, I think the biggest misconception is they think that lending to small businesses using different technology implies that those businesses are subprime. Because if they can't qualify for a bank using standard methods, that there's something wrong with the small businesses. I think that's one of the biggest misconceptions.

            Two, customers like going to the branches and talking to bankers.

Dudley: How are the banks funneling clients to the platform, to the software? Are they getting inbound leads like they normally do, and then saying, "Hey, apply here." Or are they out prospecting and acquiring new customers? A combination of the two?

Jorge: Their web site, and leads coming in from the branches. Some get leads through SEO/SEM and brokers.

Dudley: In terms of driving new relationships to the bank, from what you've seen, how are the customer acquisition cost, lifetime values, stickiness? These potential new clients that are coming through this funnel, are they moving deposits over?

Jorge: That's too early for me to say.

Dudley: It makes a ton of sense to me. Within these banks, in terms of the platform impacting their overhead (e.g. loan officers, underwriters), is it a situation where they can reposition personnel to deal with more complex loans? Is it an opportunity to make the bank more lean, to improve net interest margin, both?

Jorge: Basically, yes. We get rid of basic tasks that take a ton of time but add little value to the lending decision. Now expensive employees can be put to work on other more value-added activities.

Dudley: The slow no.

Jorge: It's crazy. You're a small business owner. Why is it taking me this long? And, by the way, it takes exactly the same amount of time it takes to do a $25,000 loan as it does a $500,000 loan.

              It shouldn't be that way. It should be, within two days, you should know. Even less. In fact, many of these loans, you should know in thirty seconds. It's about becoming a lot more efficient, and also redeploying. You can increase the customer experience by simply being a lot smarter in terms of the way you interact with your customers.

Dudley: I think it's fascinating because there's been numerous conversations I've had with banks and they say, "Look, for us to make a $50,000 loan will cost as much as it does to make a $1,000,000 loan."

But then, even dig down deeper. In terms of their loan book and diversification and volatility of their portfolio, they're being forced by their overhead and cost structure to make fewer, but larger loans. That, I speculate, brings unneeded volatility to their loan book. The whole concept resonates.

In terms of your growth, is it scaling the customer base? Are there similar adjacencies with alternative lenders or both? How does the future look for you?

Jorge: That's exactly it: Just getting more customers is proof of concept. Lenders are our customer base. Banking companies, merchant processors, like Amazon, could be our clients. Like I said, we're basically doing lending-in-a-box. Obviously, the natural target is the banking industry. They are the biggest lenders, or the most numerous, anyway. But, yes. That's the goal.

Dudley: Your revenue model, how does it work?

Jorge: Basically, subscription.

Dudley: Playing the devil's advocate here, what's a scenario or event that would derail the momentum for this?

Jorge: Customer acceptance, I'm assuming. Banks thinking that it has no value. For us, specifically, standard stuff that everyone faces. Complications. The product doesn't work. Regulatory issues, I don't think I see any problems. I think that we help compliance because we reduce some manual processes; we create more transparency than anything. We actually help the bank become more compliant. We are regulatory friendly. Standard stuff. Competition. Not getting enough customers. Micro-level, running out of business, running out of cash before making significant progress. Standard stuff.

Dudley: Is there an overarching message you want people to know and understand?

Jorge: Yeah. There are three things that I think are key. Regulatory oversight, competition and customer buying behavior will have a significant impact in lending in the coming years and lenders that don't invest in the right technology now will be left behind.

Regulation is not going away. Regulation has become more of a data-driven process, so if you as a lender, and obviously [as] a bank, don't have an architecture to allow you to provide the data a regulator needs to see, the regulator is going to limit your ability to grow and be competitive.

Second: competition. Millions of dollars are going into redefining what lending is, how loans are made, how you interact with the customer. We have all kinds of different players. From the traditional to non-traditional, like Amazon, Goldman Sachs, OnDeck to the big banks. Top ten banks that are investing millions—Wells Fargo, Chase, B of A— so a significant level of competition in the small business space and banks that don't have a digital lending solution will become less competitive

Third, there's a massive shift in customer buying behavior. How we interact is changing. Everything is going offline to online: where we interact, how we like our information, how we like to submit our information is changing. And forcing people to do it a way they don't like to do it, simply because you don't have the ability to provide the solution that fits their needs, will make you less competitive.

Dudley: Makes sense to me.

Krista Morgan:
Co-Founder, P2Bi

www.p2bi.com

"WE HAVE FOUND an unexplored niche of the internet." What if she is right? After nearly three years of lending, P2Bi has lost $1,500 on over $350 million in loans (as of this interview).

Financing accounts receivables is not new. P2Bi's approach to it is, however. As Krista and her team began exploring the space they found that every piece of major commercial asset-based lending software was "terrible." So, P2Bi built their own system in the face of countless doubters claiming P2Bi will never be able to collect on their loans.

I would be remiss if I failed to mention Krista's involvement in Women Who Startup. Krista is an advocate for changing the face of entrepreneurship. I love this mission. My mom and wife are entrepreneurs and I am fortunate to witness and support their journey firsthand. I encourage you to visit Krista's website: www.womenwhostartup.com.

Dudley: What is P2Bi?

Krista: P2Bi is a marketplace funder that provides revolving lines of credit to growing businesses backed by AR (accounts receivable) and inventory.

Dudley: I imagine you didn't wake up one day and say, "You know what? I'm going to lend to businesses based on their AR." Can you talk to your background and the process of how you came to this idea and how you vetted the concept?

Krista: Good question. I am Canadian originally but I moved to the UK and worked in digital marketing and advertising. While I was living there, I can't remember exactly but I remember at my kitchen table one night talking about sending money back to Canada and I had gone to the banks and I was like, "Interest rates are incredibly low and yet the banks are going to charge me a fortune to borrow money here just so I can stop paying Forex," like exchange fees.

I said, "People should just be able to lend to people. That would be a great idea. Why don't we just do that? I Googled it and I thought I was a genius. It turned out I was not a genius; Zopa was a genius and because I was in the UK, there was Zopa and RateSetter. I just came across those really early platforms. This must have been 2007, really early days of the industry and because I worked in digital, I just signed up for all the newsletters and I just started paying attention.

I didn't really think about it until years later; we're talking 2011. I'm working at a big agency. I had started to feel like maybe the corporate world wasn't for me. My dad, who was living in Denver at the time, and I had come up with a couple of different business ideas and we were talking through them and he started telling me about this guy he was talking to that's doing factoring and he was like, "You know, Krista, we could help this guy raise money and then we could take the commission from that."

We've been talking about a solar company. We'll go start a solar company. I looked at it. I said, "Okay, I bet we can raise money online." I was like, "People do that now. That's a thing." I started researching it. He loves to tell a story. He tells it better than I do but I phoned him up and I was like, "Dad, we have found an unexplored niche of the internet. No one is really doing this type of lending on a platform in an online way."

It was really strange. He didn't know anything about crowdfunding. I didn't know anything about factoring. We put these two ideas together. There was receivables exchange at the time but they were doing everything on invoice-by-invoice basis. From the get-go, what we said was, "There are huge liquidity issues for investors in invoice-by-invoice financing model because you're constantly getting your cash back. You have all this drag."

It's bad for businesses because they have to upload every individual invoice. We said on our platform, we want to make it feel like a line of credit. It's easy. You upload all your invoices and then you can just borrow against it. Investors can just be constantly buying into this flow of invoices rather than a single invoice.

Dudley: That's interesting because when you listen to the story about the founders in the space, it's a very iterative process. How you laid out that vision there, it sounds very similar to where you are today in terms of the line of credit against a collection of the receivables.

Krista: Yeah. I have to tell you, our business model today has evolved but it looks very similar to what we set out to do. It was just a lot fucking harder than we thought it would be. A lot of people are like, "How come no one else did this?" Neither of us had a background in finance. I was at marketing, ad tech, but only a tech light person and he was a sales guy and we just did it.

The underlying concept is similar. The mechanics of how we do everything and all the tech and how it has come together is different. I tell people a lot that I did not start a business because I had lived the problem. We started it because we saw this market opportunity and I wanted to do something different. Now that I have actually run a fast-growing company, I actually have a much easier time talking about customers now because I do live the problem that they face. It's really weird, isn't it?

Dudley: You went backwards on this.

Krista: Yeah, exactly.

Dudley: When I talk to people that, I would say, folks that have been in the lending industry for a long period of time, and I talk about this space, they're very skeptical. You can't originate and find lending flow off of this channel. If a traditional lender comes upon this and says, "Wait a minute, what's someone with a digital marketing background now doing accounts receivable financing?" How do you counter that skepticism?

Krista: Results, I counter it with results. I'm not joking. That's what I do. If you knew the number of people that said, "This will never work; you can't do it. You're never going to be able to collect money." I remember someone early on, an investor was saying, "You know, Krista, it's so easy to lend money but it's so hard to get paid back." I was like, "Yeah. No, I get that."

             Now we have lost $1,500. It's like nothing. We basically have a zero-loss portfolio after two-and-a-half years of doing this. Not to say that will continue forever but we're good at lending money. We are good at getting it back. Then I tell people that it's not rocket science. I tell this to our customers, "Financing is not rocket science. It's really just basic math and some basic concepts and everyone likes to make it sound really complicated but it isn't."

             Ultimately, building a successful company like this is about building a great team, a very diverse team, and by diverse I don't mean gender and ethnics; I also care about that but just diverse in that we are thirty people. We have six departments. Everyone from AR people, the credit people, the risk people to client success people to operations to sales. You have to be able to build a team of all these different skill sets and keep everyone going in the same direction with the double-sided marketplace.

It's like a logistical challenge but the nuts and bolts of it are not rocket science. I look at Elon Musk landing a rocket on a platform in the middle of the ocean: that's hard. I am not doing that. We are just using a whole lot of common sense and a customer-focused mentality to deliver better working capital that helps other businesses grow. That is what we do.

Dudley: Let's get into the mechanics of actually how this works and perhaps an example is the best way to describe it. I make widgets and I have this challenge with working capital. I have my cost of production that needs to be paid now yet I receive payment from my customer at a later date. Thus, a receivable is created. So, I have all these receivables, and I reach out to you. How does this work?

Krista: You are going to come talk to us. You fill out an online application. Our team is going to then give you a call, ask you a couple of questions based on what we see, and then we're going to put a term sheet out. Once we agree on terms we're going to go into diligence, collect a reasonable amount of documentation because it's a million dollar line of credit. We're going to collect documentation then we're going to run a bunch of background checks and do site visits, make sure that you are who you say you are. You've done what you say you've done and you're not going to run away to Bermuda once I open this line of credit for you.

Then they sign a contract that you're on-boarded into our platform and then they start borrowing. Really the process is through evolving lines so call it, I don't know, maybe invoice twice a month. Twice a month you're going to invoice and then you're going to log in to our system, upload one report with all your new invoicing. Our system will read it, update your borrowing base and say great. You have access to a million dollars. How much do you want?

Then you will say great, today I need $200,000. We will send that to you the next day, and then your customer, thirty days later, your customer is going to pay their invoice into our lock box and then we are going to log that, pay down the $200,000 that you borrowed from us and anything remaining is going to get swept back to you. Then you do it all again. For some customers, that happens every day; for some that goes every week, some once a month. It's very dependent on how they are running their business.

Dudley: The fund flows work such that your client's client actually pays you.

Krista: Correct.

Dudley: You're the first to be paid and then you net and reconcile their accounts.

Krista: Correct. We do that for two reasons. Well, let's call it three reasons. One because it really helps with getting paid back. Two, because it actually ensures that the business is paying the least amount of interest possible because their lines are paying down. What's happening is, lines paying down and we're charging on a daily interest rate. The balance goes down automatically. They pay less interest and they only borrow again if they need it. A pay down opens up availability on the line and they can decide if they actually need it or not.

It really keeps our interest payments low and it ensures that people can't really borrow more than they can get paid back, more than they can pay back. We're in the business of giving companies good working capital lines. It's not gross capital per se. It's not equity. The idea is you should have no trouble paying this back. We don't want you to overextend yourself.

Dudley: It is my understanding one of the key benefits that your clients see is the ability to aggregate various receivables as opposed to a one-off.

Krista: Correct.

Dudley: Can you speak to that a little bit? In terms of number of receivables in the sense of a range, what do you see from your clients?

Krista: We did start out on a more invoice-by-invoice, so people would upload ten invoices at a time and we would lend against them all. So we would batch them and say, "Okay. You just uploaded, I don't know, $100,000 worth of invoices. Here's $80,000 which you have to take." It's one of the evolutions on our model that we said, "This is really cumbersome as soon as you get to any kind of scale." As soon as you're doing two or three million dollars a year, you're going to often end up with a lot more invoices, and it's just a pain.

Just think about it at an invoice level. That's when we moved to what we call our X factor product, which is really a batch that you're submitting. What is actually an AR aging report to our system. We're just reading the total balance. We are saying, "Great, you have just uploaded $200,000 of AR." We don't care if it's one invoice or thirty invoices. To us, it's one report; it's one number that we are looking at.

Even though our system still knows the invoices, a customer isn't feeling that invoice-level detail, if that makes sense. We have customers that upload fifty invoices a day; we have customers that put out one invoice a week. It's all across the board; just every business model is going to want to do it a bit differently.

I would say on average, we probably have ... I don't even think I could put a number in. Yes, hard to say but we definitely have customers that range from having one invoice with us and people that have 8,000 invoices that we're funding at any one time.

Dudley: To the outsider looking at that, if a client has a thousand invoices, it's a labor-intensive management process. Can you speak to how you've leveraged the technology and the systems you've implemented? Was this even possible say ten years ago because you didn't have the technology to execute it in a cost-efficient manner that would make this capital worthwhile to the borrower?

Krista: An interesting question. The fact that we can just track and understand thousands and thousands of invoices in our system is absolutely a technology solution. It's not complicated. It's not complicated technology per se. The thing that we can do, in the end, an invoice is only as good as the customer behind the invoice. A lot of people when they think about invoice financing, they just care about the payer. As long as Costco is a good payer, then I'm fine but it's not true in my opinion. I don't think about it like that.

Our philosophy is that if you are working with a business that is growing and that is a good, well-intentioned business owner, who is running a good business than your risk is lower. As soon as you're starting to work with someone that is getting into trouble, that's where you end up with fraud. Fraud is a strong word. They would be like, "Oh, I'm just going to upload this one invoice that isn't a real invoice. I'm just going to do this one thing because I just need a little bit of extra cash."

That's really what our technology is trying to look for. You're buying 8,000 invoices. You can't manage it on invoice-by-invoice basis. You can't know if they're all good. You have to really understand the business and the trends in that business to see if something is going wrong. Then that prompts you to go and look at the invoices and make sure you feel good about that the invoices you purchased are in fact good invoices.

Truly, where we have leveraged technology is on a constant evaluation. It is like an ongoing risk monitoring of the portfolio because unlike a term loan, our loan risk is not going down over time. We're basically relending every week to the borrower like a credit card. They're drawing it all the way up again but we may have underwritten the deal a year ago and shit happens. How do we track the shit that's happened and make sure that we're still okay, they're still okay, and we still feel comfortable giving them a million dollars?

Dudley: Why don't your clients go to a bank? Why don't they get a term loan from another online lender? Why not an MCA? (merchant cash advance)

Krista: One, most of our customers, I wouldn't even say that they can't qualify. It's that the bank can usually not provide them with enough capital. The bank may say, "Great, you need $100,000, we'll give you $100,000, wonderful." Our portfolio companies are growing their top line revenue on average 50% year on year. What they're doing is they're getting $100,000 from the bank and we see this all the time, then they come to us and they say, "Hey, actually, I have a hundred but now I need $250K and the bank won't let me have it." Very normal.

They can't get it because they're not profitable enough. The banks have regulations. Cheap money is never cheap so there's always a cost to it and the cost of bank money is that we have to be very financially stable; things move slower. You can't just call them and say I need $100,000 extra dollars. It just doesn't happen. High growth companies tend to need more flexible capital and that's where people like us come into play.

In terms of other options, AR financing is generally going to be the cheapest of the alternative lending capital types. Receivable financing is usually the cheapest because it is the least risky. It is very well understood. The legal contracts for getting your money back as a lender is very strong. Just a lot of protection in this space whereas unsecure lending like MCA's, term loan I guess can be both but there just tend to be more expensive.

The other problem with the term loan and we see this all the time with business owners. If you look across our portfolio and our lines, someone has a million dollar line. They're not borrowing a million dollars every day for 365 days. Their average utilization is going to run somewhere between 50% and 65% but it's going to flex them to a 100% drawn and then it's going to go down to zero.

In a term loan, you're going to pay a lower interest rate but for a fixed amount of capital even when you don't need it. When we do the cost comparison of the money, our money is more expensive on the sticker rate but the effective cost to the business owner is usually less than a term loan for that same amount because they're only paying for what they use.

That was a fundamental philosophy of P2Bi is that we only charge people for money that they use. If you don't need the money, we don't charge you for it and then to another point about technology, we use technology to really efficiently move capital around behind the scenes so that we're also not paying for the money if you don't need it.

Dudley: With that being a segue, can you talk about the terms of the loan?

Krista: To get a 1-year term, 1.5% origination fee on the size of the line upfront and then a daily interest rate on our portfolio is going to run somewhere between 15% and 19% annualized. There is a cancellation fee in the agreement if you cancel before the first year but everything is waived if you go to a bank. Again, a core term of ours is if and when the bank decided to lend to you and you want to go to the bank, we make it very easy for you to do that. There's no minimum usage fee and you're just paying on exactly the balance of what you have drawn that day.

Dudley: You mentioned your origination points. How else does P2Bi make money?

Krista: P2Bi is a hybrid marketplace balance sheet lender, because we do have some balance sheet capital in the mix. We're the lender so our revenue is the origination fee plus the interest and then the cost of goods is the cost we're paying for capital so taking a spread. Business models take a spread between the top line, call it an average of 18% on the top line and a cost of capital just around 11%.

Dudley: Is that cost of capital being funded by the crowd?

Krista: Partly, so on any given day, this varies but about 85% of our portfolio is off balance sheet in the marketplace.

Dudley: An investor is effectively lending to you as the conduit to the account receivable financing?

Krista: The investors are participating in an asset purchase. They are actually buying a small proportional piece of every receivable that is in a given loan. They invest loan by loan. There's no pool and what they own is a proportional share of the underlying assets that have been lent against.

Dudley: What do the investors' return profile look like?

Krista: It's about 11%.

Dudley: Then they would be earning 11%. You may be charging 20% and that's your spread?

Krista: Correct. We don't charge 20%, just to be clear. Our average on the portfolio is about 18%.

Dudley: Okay, thank you for the clarity. In terms of the borrower, how are you underwriting these clients and finding them because you mentioned the revenue increasing 50% year over year. That's pretty extraordinary.

Krista: Yeah, it's more common than you might think especially in a consumer product company. We see it all the time. Someone has a $100,000 revenue and then Costco picks them up. The next thing you know they're doing two-and-a-half million just at Costco. It can happen pretty quickly.

We have credit policy. Is this a borrower that fits our profile? Can we get comfortable? We like to be in senior secured position. We like to have personal guarantees. We like there to be good growth in revenue. They don't have to be cash flow positive but we like to see a path there. Those are probably the major criteria. No significant tax issues or personal criminal issues. All those typical things.

Then in terms of how we find them, it's a lot of referrals, partners and just word of mouth. We have a direct team as well that's going out. For example, we're very well known in the natural foods industry so we speak at trade shows and we go and we have a very good reputation there. We do some direct work as well. Unlike some of the other marketplace lenders doing million dollar deals, I believe our entire target market is give or take a million businesses.

We're not lending to restaurants and very main street businesses. These are consumer product professional services, manufacturing, distribution companies that need capital and you have a million dollars in revenue already. We try to be much more targeted in our go-to market and we can build a billion dollar portfolio with 3,000 customers. It's not mass market in the way Lending Club and even, I think, Funding Circle and OnDeck are to a greater extent.

Dudley: You keep using the million as a proxy but in terms of the size of the credit facilities what is the range?

Krista: Minimum $250,000; our max is five million—but then we did a ten million dollar deal last month or last quarter so ten million—but I think our average really is about a million dollars if you looked across a portfolio.

Dudley: Are you cleaning up inefficiencies within a market that existed before? You had already mentioned you weren't finding it in the online channel but offline, old bricks and mortar, are you creating a whole new business because you're using technology to bring transparency to a sub-market that didn't exist or are you just making an existing market more efficient? What is your spot here?

Krista: The receivables financing market: several hundred billion dollars and is it inefficient? Yes. Here's what I'll say. I think about it in terms of this: if you need a $50,000 loan, it's pretty easy these days. You go to Kabbage and have $50,000 in seven minutes.

It's amazing. If I need a million dollars, it is really fucking complicated. I'm talking to banks. I'm talking to alternative lenders. I'm thinking about concentration limits; there's all this paperwork.

The software: we've seen every piece of major commercial significant asset-based lending software and it is terrible. It was so terrible that we realized that there was no way we could build our business if we didn't build our own platform. It's just clunky and it's all the things you just mentioned. It wasn't transparent. It was impossible to figure out what you were paying as a borrower and it even made our operations less efficient by trying to move to some of these back office systems that have not been built in the last couple of years.

UX (user experience), what we expect of our software has changed in the last five years; very different to how it was ten years ago. I would say, as a business, our goal is [to make] getting a million dollars as easy as it is to get $50,000 and then to really be able to scale with a business as it grows. I want our product to feel like it's as easy as a credit card. The money is there as you need it and then we fade into the background. Yes, technology is hugely critical to delivering that customer experience.

I would not say we're there yet. We're just a lot further along than most of the other people. Truly the thing that we are disrupting that a lot of people don't necessarily realize in the marketplace lending model is every commercial lender is lending off of a balance sheet. A certain amount of equity, they're levering it; they have really cheap capital but it is one fixed into constraint in terms of concentration and you can't hold an invoice after ninety days.

The entire alternative lending world works on these levered warehouse lines. It means that they're not flexible. They cannot grow. What is amazing about our platform with the marketplace is that our marketplace, there's no leverage ratio. If we could find fifty customers tomorrow that needed a million dollars, we don't need more equity to get that funded. We can just open up those deals in our marketplace and get them done. That ability of scaling capital is a huge differentiator especially in the commercial lending market.

Then, when you think about the technology we've built. One of my favorite customers, he's in Albany. He owns a staffing company. He has $5 million with us. He has $5 million and he only sells to a huge healthcare company. He went around to all these factoring, alternative lenders. His business is profitable. He's been doing it for a while and everyone turned him down because they were, "We can't take $5 million of concentration risk to one payer." It just wasn't going to happen.

Our marketplace model means we are automatically diversifying risk. We have on average 150 investors in every loan. No single person is taking on all the risk and that means we can do things that other commercial lenders can't do. Syndication is not a new thing in the commercial lending world but doing it at this micro level is only possible with technology. It is hard for me to say we're the only but we are one of the only people that can do a line of that size and syndicate it at this micro level at the speed that we do it.

Dudley: That's a phenomenal point and I think that's why you and I sit and look at this and are so bullish on it. With that being said, how does this go bad? What would happen that the skeptics say I told you so?

Krista: It's funny, I remember when I was at a VC fundraising which we never raised. There's this whole long story about not raising VC funding but I went and talked to VC after VC and there was one VC like, "What's going to happen if your entire portfolio crashes overnight and this market goes down?" I was like, "You know, that doesn't really happen." If you look historically, very unlikely. Remember, our portfolio is extremely diversified with all these companies.

Then within companies you have all these invoices and then within that you have all these investors who only have a small percentage of the risk. It's an extremely diversified model. The risk has been syndicated in a lot of levels. What we would expect to happen in a downturn is that people stop having AR. We're lending against AR so if Costco is not buying from me anymore, our portfolio contracts because our customers just won't have as many assets. Also, we may have slow payment issues.

It's not going to happen overnight. Some crazy black swan event would have to come up for it to just happen overnight. When I talk to guys in the factoring industry who have been through 2008, they say actually, the banks, they dropped their C&I (commercial and industrial) portfolio. C&I lending tanked in 2008, 2009 and so what happened is all these companies came out of the banks and they needed alternative financing. It's actually a reasonable time for us.

Not that I would ever wish market downturn but there's actually a lot of opportunity when the banks contract their C&I lending. There are still businesses. They still need capital and if anything, working capital becomes more important because I think people are going to slow pay. Back to my earlier point about ongoing risk monitoring. The thing that will make or break our success as a platform is: Do we have an extremely robust way to monitor the health of our customers, their payers and the quality of the AR and assets that we are buying?

Again, it's not rocket science. It just takes a lot of common sense. We just have a lot more variables to look at and we pull those together into models and we analyze it. I'm not concerned. I actually believe that we are a far better place to handle a recession than your average balance sheet lender.

Dudley: Is there an overarching message you want to get across? If there's one thing you want to communicate, what would that be?

Krista: I'm trying to think what my big soap box issues are. The things I care about. In my mind, what we just talked about. The way you think about risk changes so you can do syndication. Even with our most sophisticated institutional investors: they say they would rather invest in a million dollar credit than a ten million dollar credit. I always find it fascinating.

The company that can justify $10 million has $10 million of assets to lend against, is a far better company, really, and you can just put a $100,000 up to buy in to this security of a $10 million credit. Risk changes and I think we don't fully understand what it means and we're still thinking about risk in an old way.

I think just encourage people to think differently about it because being much more diversified does make a difference. Now my job is just figuring out how to quantify that. My other issues all are on diversity but I don't really think that matters in this book. I don't know how many female founders you've gotten to interview but certainly, we need more women in finance.

Dudley: It's an interesting segue. As I mentioned earlier, I think your product is really compelling but I think we both recognize there are not only many female founders in this space but in general. Using that to talk about Women Who Start Up and your role and supporting the ecosystem, and encouraging other women to take a path like you've taken it, can you speak to Women Who Start Up and your role and goals? I do think it plays a part so I definitely wanted to cover it.

Krista: I am so glad. Women Who Start Up is really just about making sure that we tell a story as a female entrepreneur because they don't get told as often. You just don't see them as often and all the data shows that women run great businesses. I could tell you the number of people, mainly men who said to me, "I can't believe you started this business. How did you learn about finance?" In that way, how did you learn about this? I'm like, "I can read and understand shit."

What I'm trying to tell women is that it doesn't matter. I started this business that I have no business starting; but again to my earlier point, I think what makes a marketplace lending platform work, there's some basics. You need trust and you need integrity and you need to always be thinking you are living your life in a balance. I live my life asking what's good for a borrower and what's good for our investors. I'm trying to find a win-win all the time and a lot of business is like that, and actually women are great at that.

I can hire really smart finance people. I have hired them. They're wonderful. They know a lot of shit I don't know but that's not what you need to start this business, any business. You have to build a team. You have to tell your story. You have to balance a lot of competing interests and it's not that fucking hard, really and truly and people I think make it out to be more than it is. So that's my soap box.

Jason Fritton:
Founder, Patch of Land

www.patchofland.com

A S OF THE interview Patch of Land has executed nearly $200 million in originations across 33 states. In the spring of 2016, Patch announced a commitment from a large credit fund to purchase up to $250 million in loans.

When vetting the Patch of Land idea, Jason was told by his attorney he would go to prison because he was publicly soliciting securities. He was told by a large Chicago broker he was ridiculous because nobody is interested in raising capital and investing in real estate via an online marketplace. In short, the professionals did not like the idea. "It is not how real estate is done."

Jason followed through anyway. Patch launched their first loan of $120,400 and optimistically expected the crowd to take thirty days to fund it. The first loan funded in two days. A platform was born.

Dudley: What is Patch of Land?

Jason :   Patch of Land, at its core, is a real estate crowd
               funding company. That's how we started. We've
               expanded to be more of a marketplace lender these
               days. One of our biggest assets, one of our biggest
               advantages is our very large, very powerful, very
               loyal user base. We have the entire spectrum of
               crowd investors on the site at this point. You got
               everyone from boomers that have made a good
               amount of capital over their lifetime, to Google
               execs. I have one managing director of one of the
               largest banking consortiums in the world on the
               site. And everybody in between. We've been able to
               utilize that to really bring a level of transparency,
               daylight, flexibility and breadth into commercial
               real estate lending, something that hasn't yet existed
               before. Massive market but a very insular, very
               antiquated market.

Dudley: If I'm coming to your site for the first time, if I just
               heard about Patch of Land, what can I expect to
               find? You mentioned it is real estate crowd funding,
               but what exactly are you doing?

Jason :   If you were coming to the site for the first time, I
               would expect and hope that you would find very
               clear, very easy, immediate access to investment and
               an asset class that perhaps you hadn't had access to
               before, to be able to invest in real estate. We've made
               real estate approachable online. When in the past,
               it's been deals in back rooms or Excel spreadsheets
               or handshakes. Now we've brought business online.
               I would expect, as an investor, to be able to access

very high quality real estate opportunities from your coach, mobile phone, from your pajamas. If you were a real estate professional looking to gain capital, I would expect you to be able to clearly and easily access a much wider network of investors and available capital than you've ever had access to in the past.

Dudley: You mentioned it a couple times: it's a new way to look at the capital raising business for investors and for sponsors. Where did the idea come from? Do you remember where you were? The Eureka moment when you said, "This is a great concept. I have to create this thing."

Jason :   I do. I'm going to be embarrassed to tell you how it started though. I don't know if I told you in the past, but I ran a company before and did very well with that until the financial crash. I lost it, and lost everything. I went from owning a $30 million company to owning literally nothing overnight. That's the risk you take as an entrepreneur and a business owner. Once you do it, that's really all you do for the rest of your life. You could take a day job here and there. Once that's in your blood, that's pretty much what you fight for the rest of your productive life anyhow.

After I lost my previous company, I sat down and I just got out a pad of paper and just started putting ideas down on it. Honestly, I just brainstormed on my couch. I'd known the CEO of a company that did crowd-sourced graphic design. It wasn't crowd funding but it was crowd sourcing, and was just blowing up the entire industry. Very powerful. Disrupting everything. I thought that that's really where all of this was going. I was amazed by how powerful that really was. The ability to be able to take thousands of people you never really met before and be able to focus them on a common goal, on a common direction. Be able to accomplish something with that large group of people easily that it would have been very difficult or even impossible before by yourself or with a small group of people. To be able to make that scalable, they were doing that.

I really wanted to look at how I could add value doing the same thing. How I could get the crowd together to accomplish something difficult. Where does this add value? Where is it not being currently done? Real estate resonates with people deep down. Everybody wants to feel that they own a piece of the planet, or in this case, a patch of land. I was trying to figure out how to make that work. Honestly, my first iteration of this, the thing I marked down on that piece of paper was really just patches of land. I was looking to crowd fund different little patches of land so people could really say that they own a piece of the planet. They got an acre in the rainforest or something like that. It really was a lame idea to begin with. There's no revenue stream in that. It was a blind brainstorm.

I wrote fifty ideas down on that piece of paper. As soon as I put that down, everything else just went out the window. I really fixed on it because I knew that there was something there. Over the course of that afternoon, I refined it to say we could actually acquire real property and do something good with it. I remember I went with my family to take a trip to go see my parents. I was with my brother who was in Chicago with me at the time. I just couldn't stop talking about it and I had a bit of a cold. By the time I got to my parents' house, I had no voice left whatsoever. My brother was just exasperated from listening to me talking about it. He was pretty glad that I had lost my voice at that point.

I got back to Chicago; I started going to the auctions out there to see. I'm not a real estate guy. At this point, I was just a tech guy. I wanted to see what was available. I'm sure I've told you this story before, but I went to the different auctions. There was always the same group of people there. They all knew each other. Everyone was on a first name basis. They're all relatively wealthy, accomplished, brilliant people. Always just the same people. They were buying up the big properties. The $50 million properties for $5 million. This was back in 2010. The market had cratered at that point. You're in Chicago. [Dudley the interviewer is located in Chicago.] You know what the real estate market was like back then. Banks weren't lending and there was just a wasteland.

A property came up for auction in the Lakeview neighborhood. It was nicer than the property I was living in. The minimum bid on it was $20,000. Nicer property than I was living in, in Chicago, a nice neighborhood, for $20,000. Nobody bid on it. Nobody touched it. The people that had the skills, the experience and the resources were going after the big properties. The people that didn't have the resources, didn't have the capital originally, weren't getting it from anywhere else. I said, "This is a real opportunity." This property was tagged, the windows were busted, glass in the yard. It was dragging down property values of everything around it. Generally, a danger for the neighborhood.

I went to my attorney. I said, "This is a big opportunity. I'm going to find local artisans and contractors and professionals to make this place nice again, to be able to acquire it and to invest in it. I want to find people that believe the same way I do online. We're going to focus them together in a systematic way to be able to acquire and manage property and eventually do something good for the community and still see a lucrative investment return." Which is not an easy thing to find. It's not easy to make money and also do something good too.

My attorney said, "That's a great idea. I love that idea. I would invest in that, but if you do it, you're going to prison. It's public solicitation of security. You can't just go online to people that you don't know and tell them to invest in something."

I tend to be a very stubborn person, so I found Congressman McHenry and Congressman Dover, co-sponsoring what became the crowd funding exemption of 2012 JOBS Act. I worked a lot of phones to get people interested, lent my support. I still think there's a video of Patch of Land fluttering around the legislature somewhere. We did get the interest. We really had good buyer support in this. The Republicans loved it for a whole set of reasons. The Democrats loved it for a whole different set of reasons. The president indicated his willingness to sign the bill.

That's when I really put together Patch of Land seriously as far as we put a team together, an incubator space above Merchandise Mart out there in Chicago, the 1871 incubator. I worked my day job until 7:00 at night and I would take the train to Merchandise Mart there. I think the last train was like 11:30 or something like that. There were a lot of times when I took a cab home. Did that pretty much every night.

Dudley: You had this concept, you had the hypothesis. How did you test the hypothesis? What were the first things you did? That first loan, how did it look? How did you acquire the borrower and what was the project like?

Jason :   I tried to test it long before I got the first loan. Probably not the way to go about it, but I found the professionals. I went to a broker office in Chicago and basically gave her my best pitch. I remember rehearsing for it and trying it out. She was visibly, noticeably angry at the entire concept. She asked me to leave her office. She could not believe that anyone would be interested in something so ridiculous. I got thrown out of a couple of securities attorneys' offices. Thought there was no way it could happen.

There is a lady that was teaching about real estate. I brought her the concept. She was the only one that really liked it, early days. Even my now-partner and brother didn't like it at first. He made me do a whole lot of proving of the concept before he came on board. When I first started, I just thought I would go to the professionals and none of the professionals liked it. That wasn't how real estate was done. Depending upon who you talk to, that was either one of the biggest indicators of the challenges I was going to face in trying to get this business running, or one of the best indicators that it was going to happen.

We put together how the model would look, which is a fancy word of saying we guessed a whole lot of how we would really like this thing to go. We put together a lot of different marketing materials. We put together some tech demos. Went out and showed anybody that would look. Eventually, we got some decent traction. A seasoned investor from a prominent family here in Beverly Hills saw us and reached out and really liked the concept and said, "If you move the team to LA, I'll provide the seed funding." Better than that, he also provided a credit line for us to start acquiring the properties and making the loans.

One of the biggest issues, one of the issues that all crowd funders are going to see, is the chicken and the egg argument. How do you find quality product if you don't have the investors ready and willing and set to go to invest in it? How are you going to find the investors if you don't have a product? With this, we were able to bypass that. We used internal capital to make our first little loan, $120,400. That was our first loan. We launched that in October of 2013. Roughly three weeks after we got out to Los Angeles.

We expected it to take about thirty days or so to fund. We think we were maybe a little bit optimistic at that point. For $120,000, if people are putting in little bits of money here and there, it could take a month to fund. We funded it in less than two days. We were actually at a crowd funding conference. We launched it right before we got in the car to go to the conference and it was funded by the time we got back in the car to head home.

We had no other properties to fund in the meantime. We had nothing up on the site. Nobody knew about us yet. We had a bunch of investors that apparently really had the appetite for something like this. We didn't have any additional products. We really had to crunch to move on to the next one.

Dudley: How did that loan turn out?

Jason :   Good. We actually did it on time, on schedule. Again, I'm not a real estate guy, but if our first project fails, there's no recovering. I wanted to find something that was as much of a no-brainer as possible. We found the president of a real estate investment club who was also a high-networked individual who was also a real estate attorney who also did tons of investing on his own in New Jersey. Very credit-worthy borrower as well. He just did us a favor by letting us fund that first deal.

Dudley: When you look at loans today, can you speak about your underwriting process and how you go about vetting the sponsors? How do you balance between vetting the individual that's managing the projects and the actual value of the property itself?

Jason : We know a lot of private lenders that will focus only on the asset because in a worst case scenario, they can take the asset back. I know a lot of private money lenders that focus only on the borrower, because if you make good loans to good people, the rest of it works out as long as you meet some basic minimum criteria. We're really a hybrid approach. We like to be able to work with experienced professionals with a good reasonable expectation and be able to pull off the projects on time and on budget. We really look deeply in the underlying property as well.

We'll do your traditional real estate underwriting. We'll do a full walk-through appraisal, arm's length appraisal. The appraiser will give us a "subject to" and do an "as is" value from a licensed real estate appraiser. We used that as our baseline if we take a look at all of the information we have access to internally. We're able to tap into a great deal of additional resources between the MLS and RealtyTrac and Onboard Informatics and everything on top of that. We were able to get a great deal of data. We take that data and we structure it and we provide it to our on-staff underwriters.

We have a set of guidelines, depending upon the property type and the project type. Whether it is a fix and flip, a purchase construction, a rate and term refi (refinance), whether it is a rent property. We have different guidelines for whether it is single family residential and whether it is midsized multi family or large multi family, an office space. We've even done hotels.

We learned quickly to get very experienced, very professional people to be able to help us develop good, standardized guidelines for the underwriting itself so that we're operating under a scalable approach. If we had to iterate on those guidelines and we're able to, at least we have those guidelines. They've worked out well for us. As of today's date, we've done hundreds of loans, nearly $200 million worth of origination over several years, in 33 states, very different property types, very different markets. We've never lost anybody's money yet.

Dudley: Critics of this model would say that real estate is local. It's location, location, location. We all know empirically that one side of the street can be different than the other side of the street. How does Patch of Land keep this in perspective and gain that local perspective and have that understanding?

Jason :   I would say those people are absolutely correct, but information isn't the sole domain of our own mind. We can get access to that information.

Dudley, I know you do. You probably know which neighborhoods not to invest in. There's too much crime there or properties sit too long in that particular area or there's a problem down the street or the neighborhood has been going downhill for whatever reason or the gangs are moving in. Whatever it actually may be.

My proposal to you is that I'm also able to find that information. I can take a look at heat maps as far as crime is concerned. I can take a look at the ratio of grocery stores to liquor stores in that particular neighborhood. I can take a look at the bike path. I can take a look at real estate mainstays, time on market, average rent rolls, average price for that zip code. Take a look at the sub zip codes and see what's there. We can see what has traditionally been part of real estate underwriting, which is go to the comps themselves and how far apart or similar they actually are. We can take a look at what the construction budget calls for and what the average price per square foot value gain is on that [property] in that particular area.

We can aggregate that data quickly and then we use our baseline, which is the appraisal. If we have too much variance from that baseline, we don't have to do the deal. If we had too much variance and we still consider doing the deal, it goes to credit committee. We have very experienced people that sit on credit committee to hash over the deal and make those decisions. We will, to put it bluntly, make some bad decisions. If I'm making mostly good decisions in a very wide area and my crowd investors are able to diversify instead of putting tons of money into a single deal, they can invest smaller amounts of money in a large variety of deals, then our performance gets to be very predictable and reliable. We get to have the market opportunity that a local lender, a local real estate professional, wouldn't always have. Does that make sense?

Dudley: Absolutely. I love the big data in this industry because there's so much data on it.

Jason :   It's getting better.

Dudley: Yeah, getting a lot better and will continue to.

Jason :   As they bring the county records online, as we take a look at ways to very quickly and cheaply get UCC search information, as we're really able to get those micro market pin points, data points on individual properties, we're going to continue to make better decisions. That's not to say that I'm ever going to get to a point where maybe the decision that I'm able to make is as good as a Dudley in his own neighborhood, in his own hometown, would be able to make. If I can get it close, and I have the advantage of being able to lend hundred thousands of sub markets across the country to where our gains vastly outnumber our losses and our investors are well diversified, overall, we're going to have a really good result.

Dudley: Absolutely. To mention nothing if you get it close and the equity that a sponsor has put in the deal, the margin of error that equity provides is a nice benefit for the investor. When you're wrong, which invariably happens, you have the protection in there that it's not a big "whammy."

Jason :   Right, there's some downside protection. We're covered just in case. We're not investing in somebody's amorphous concept. We're not investing in somebody's unrealized idea of something that could be great down the road. We're investing in hard assets. At the very least, there's something you can go throw a rock at.

Dudley: Who is Patch of Land replacing in the market? Is this a new industry or is it an innovation on an existing industry?

Jason :   It's an innovation and a disruption on an existing industry. The industry is huge. Hundred billion dollars a year alone on the fix and flip market. You mix in small balance and commercial, you're in the trillions. You mix in the rental portfolios, you're in the trillions. Massive industry but still an antiquated one. At the beginning, we're replacing those frontlines within the industry. The existing private money lenders, the smaller mom-and-pops that exist very locally that maybe don't have the range of underwriting or the range of credit box and products that we have. They don't have the breadth of credit supply that we have or the ability to process the volume that we do.

I actually just got off the phone a little bit ago with an existing private money lender out of

Miami. He's not one of the really small ones. He does about $60 million a year when Miami was back from this upswing. A decent amount of capital there. He's in his mid-60s and likes to hunt and fish. Does not like going out to the meet ups and everything else to try and source deals and underwrite them and do the docs and look at the taxes and the insurance and everything. Now he found that he can just send funds to our portal on a diversified basis and actually make pretty much the same or better returns that he was making before doing the lending himself. He's able to see double digit returns, again secured by the hard asset. He doesn't have to do all the work. He clicks a button on his phone and invests in property in Miami.

That's actually what we're working with him now on. Making sure he's got good high volume account that he can invest easily with us. He's not a tech-enabled investor. He is roughly sixty-five and has his calculations and the expanse of technology exists of an Excel spreadsheet or Outlook. We're really—I don't want to say displacing, but maybe accentuating now at this point. As we continue to be able to lend across the credit spectrum, once we bring on more of the institutional firepower, different hedge funds and pension funds and so on to where we can actually really lend on much lower rate but higher grade paper, at the same time be able to utilize the power of our crowd for the other touch of products. We're working to be able to become more of a holistic, one-stop shop for real estate lending. That type of flexibility is really powerful.

Dudley: You mentioned supply of credit. In terms of dollar amounts of applications you receive on the platform in a given month, what are you seeing in a given month?

Jason : The application volume itself?

Dudley: What comes into the funnel?

Jason : Upwards of a half billion.

Dudley: A month? That's amazing.

Jason : Thank you. Not all of them are good. In fact most of them are not. It is opportunity flow.

Dudley: That's a good way the put it. You obviously filter through that. In February [2016], you announced that you got a $250 million commitment from a credit fund. Could you talk about that and the impact on not only Patch of Land but more broadly the real estate crowd funding industry and what that means?

Jason : That was actually early back then. We worked out an MLPA with them or if we could meet within a certain credit guideline, we can expect them to purchase on a whole note basis. These folks don't exist alongside the crowd. They exist outside of the crowd. It's much more difficult to find the institutional buyers that will buy fractionally in individual deals, though we have some now, which is good. This group was huge for our growth. Not only that, but just huge for showing that we could do it to the rest of Wall Street essentially. Now they're beating down our doors.

We haven't signed the docs yet. We're looking for another $250 to $500 [million] from a very well-respected group that's been in real estate for a very long time. We've got a total pipeline volume on the institutional side of about $1.2 billion annually. Not that it's signed up yet but that's what's actually looking to get on board. They just keep coming. Everybody is looking to get access to this type of product, this type of asset class. That first group is really key. We're able to show that we could make it successful, we could make it scalable, we could make it systematic. Now we can use the template for some of the other folks.

Dudley: Some of the institutional investors you've mentioned, what's their push back? What is keeping them from saying, "This is definitely a channel for us. We want to attack it."

Jason :   There's a lot of different concerns. There's concentration concerns. We're not doing $6,000 Lending Club loans. We're doing $600,000 mortgages essentially. There's always the concern that they're putting too much. They're not going to work with us fractionally in most cases. They want the whole notes. For a lot of funds, that's a particular risk. How much they're investing to a particular note, into a particular borrower, into a particular market, into particular products. Everyone is still a little bit gun-shy at real estate too. They want to make sure that we're not just giving loans out to anybody that can fog a mirror, that we do have robust underwriting guidelines and policies. That we have good asset management and work out policies and collection policies.

Wednesday or Thursday of last week, we had to undergo a full audit of everything that we do. All the way from how we source the different opportunities and qualify the different opportunities to get them to processing, to get them to underwriting, to get them to finance and legal and closing then post-closing then get the documents over and collateral transfer, what controls we have in place. All the way to what the mission of the company actually is, how I started it. We went through everything on that. The response was highly positive. Stressful time.

They're looking to deploy up to $20 million plus a month. We are still a new, young company. They want to be able to see that everything is bolted down. We have the ability to pull it off, that we're not going away any time soon. Everybody has different criteria. It's hard to say there's push back across several different fronts depending upon the nature of their funds, whether it's an evergreen or closed end fund or how long we can do a project, what the actual term is, what type of product and type of asset classes. A lot of times they're either underwritten by Deutsche or Credit Suisse and they have to be able to follow the requirements set from there. A lot of them have leverage and what's required on top of that. There has to be an exception process as well. There's so many different factors that sometimes it doesn't fit in well within a few straightforward guidelines. There needs to be an exception process and how it's documented. There's been an enormous amount of work, let's just say that.

Now it's a company asset. It's one of those things where people in VC will ask me, "What's going to stop somebody from just popping up and doing what you do?" I say, "Good luck. It doesn't matter how much money you have. There's only so quickly you can get these things nailed down; you can get these processes put together and documented and tested and you got the control environments in place and you get the people hired." It's not an easy thing, especially with real estate.

Dudley: Let's play devil's advocate. Why wouldn't this work? Is there an event or something that keeps you up at night that would derail this so to speak?

Jason :   I'm worried about the black swan event. When I lost my first company, the reason I lost everything ... I was effectively homeless. I put in everything that I had. I sold my car for cash to make payroll because I thought that there's no way this event would be this huge. It's coming back. This is a correction. This is just a quick change, a short localized recession and then everything is coming back. I didn't realize it was going to be a massive horrible event. Worst economic event we've seen since the Great Depression. We don't want to see that again. Having lived through that once, I don't want to live through that again.

Part of what I do every day is to come up with redundancy plans, contingency plans to make sure that if something terrible does happen, that my staff is going to be okay, that my family is going to be okay and the company is going to be okay, that my investors are going to be okay. That's why we put into place this trustee and custodian bank that's been around for a couple hundred years. If we get hit by a meteor tomorrow, they'll be able to manage our investors' commitments. That worries me. I don't expect a meltdown like what we saw before. I do expect to see a correction. I do expect to see localized downturns that may combine together to get a widespread downturn. I expect to have a plan and a product and both a demand source and a supply source to be able to meet that particular challenge.

One of the things you have to expect with running a small business or starting a business is that you have no idea what's going to happen. We have a situation where we did a very big loan. We did everything right. Everything right. Check post-closing and we found out that a regulation had been passed in that particular state that the title company that was closing the property didn't take into effect and that our multi-million dollar loan did not have a lien. It was really an unsecured multi-million dollar loan. The attorney who was handling it for the title company simply missed it. We did everything right on our side. We could have gone after the E&L insurance fee of the attorney and so on, but it was a multi-million dollar loan and the E&L insurance is only for a million. What happens to the rest of it?

Luckily, we were able to work through that. We were able to get our lien secured. Something terrible could have happened there. That's always true with any new business. We put a control environment in place for that. Every time one of these happens, you find a way to deal with it. You find a way to make it work, to protect the people you're supposed to protect and then to make sure it doesn't happen again. Or at least not the same way. There's always a concern that a huge problem comes up you wish you could have foreseen but didn't. It's just too much for you. I think that's really why most small businesses do not succeed. Something happens that comes out the left field that nobody expects and they just don't find a way out of it in time.

That keeps me up. There's always the concern of just something happening with the product, or is there a widespread scare where the majority of our capital source, which is the crowd, the majority of our user base, the majority of our value as a company itself decides not to invest with us anymore. Do we have a Lending Club situation? That's scary as well. The best you can do is try and plan for it as much as possible. Be transparent; be open and try and fix problems when it happens.

Dudley: How early is this market—real estate crowd funding—if you had to offer a prediction? Also, if you have any bold predictions in that crystal ball of yours in terms of the industry and if you were to look at this thing five, ten years forward?

Jason: I would say that we're just getting started, honestly. We're in the very infancy of what this actually is in a massive market that is almost completely offline and we're bringing online. We're looking to do up to, this year, a quarter billion and that is nothing. There are branches of Bank of America that do more business than that. I'm sorry—almost every branch of Bank of America does more business than that. This is, however, is going to be the direction the economy takes as people get more connected, as access becomes more easy and more exotic. Not even exotic, but more harder-to-reach asset classes and opportunities. As the regulations and the legislative environment allows for more flexibility in how we work with investors and who we can work with, it's just going to blow wide open.

Right now we can only work with accredited investors except in our certain highly controlled situations, which almost make it not worth going to a non-accredited. I truly believe that you shouldn't have to drive a Mercedes to be able to make an informed investment on your own behalf. I know brilliant people who do not meet the accredited threshold. I know people who are easily above that threshold that have millions and millions of dollars that probably should not be investing. That's the direction that the economy is taking.

Dudley: Is there any theme or anything you'd want to communicate on a high level basis, a point you wanted to get across?

Jason: I would say that: look for yourself. That's part of the fun and the power of this particular type of vehicle, this particular type of channel. You can just go online and look. It's all visible. It's there. It's out of the backroom. It's out of the smoke-filled brokerage houses. It's online for everybody to see. Go check it out. You can find the information that you're looking for. You look at how we've done in the past and everybody can do that. That's what I would say. I would say, if you have any interest whatsoever, everything is out there in full daylight and for everybody to take a look at. If you're not seeing something you need, let me know and I'll find it for you.

Peter Renton:
Founder, Lend Academy

www.lendacademy.com

www.lendit.com

Before SoFi advertised during the Super Bowl, they first advertised at LendIt. Peter is an investor who turned a blog into a podcast and a conference spanning three continents and thousands of attendees.

Peter did not come from a lending background. After selling his printing business he was looking for someplace to invest the proceeds. With rates at the time near 0% his options, like ours, were limited. Upon finding Prosper and Lending Club he became hooked.

I encourage you to check out his conference, podcast and blog. In Peter's eyes consumer and small business credit belongs in everyone's portfolio. As you would probably guess, he believes all lending is moving online.

Dudley: It's my understanding prior to the P2P space, you
           owned a printing business and had sold. Can you
           start there on your journey, about how you came to
           this and you thought, "Oh, man, this is a great idea.
           I have to get involved."

Peter :   I was in the printing business, in fact I had sold my
           second company in 2008 just before the financial
           crisis and I watched interest rates go down to zero.
           I had a large amount of cash that I was looking to
           invest. I read an article about Prosper in I think
           it was Money Magazine. I don't have the original
           article, but I think it was Money Magazine. I took
           it out and I thought, "That sounds like a really
           good idea. With interest rates down to zero let me
           dabble and put some money into that." By the time
           I got around to it, Prosper was in a quiet period so
           I ended up discovering Lending Club and opened
           up an account with them. This was 2009 now, and I
           just loved the whole idea of it: loved the simplicity,
           loved the yield, loved the premise of, you know, just
           making things more efficient in and being able to,
           as you said, be my own bank kind of thing. All of
           that was very appealing to me.

           I just started to invest and continued to sort of
           pay attention. Didn't really think that I was going
           to make this my career, but I was looking for
           something new to do. I took a couple years off after
           selling my last business and then I was looking for
           something new to do and this just kept on coming
           up to me and I ended up finding a website that was
           actually for sale that was based on this space. It was

really just an affiliate marketing play, so I bought that website and I started writing.

When I did my research, I was astounded that no one was writing about this space on a regular basis. No one was covering it as a blogger or what have you in this country. [Peter is from Australia.] A few had been but they'd stopped and so I basically had the market to myself. I started writing about it, started just to develop a small following. With that I was able to develop relationships with the leading platforms. You know, it was a small industry back then and I could easily go and get a phone call with the CEO of any of the platforms and this really just basically was an enthusiast in the space.

It wasn't really until conference got started that things started to take off, and that was back in 2013. It was funny because it was my New Year's resolution to start a conference because my readers had told me, "It would be great if we could all get together in person. You should start a conference." You know, I'd never put on a conference before, but it was in the back of my mind that I should sort of explore that avenue. Then, literally like January 7th or whatever, I got an email from my now-partners saying, "Are you interested in putting on a conference?" We all got together. We liked each other. We felt like we could work well together and we put on the first LendIt conference in New York in—what was that?—June of 2013. Since then it's taken off and these days, I do a little bit of writing but the majority of my time is spent on this conference business.

Dudley: When you bought Social Lending, the website, why was that the move? What in your past or what in your business experiences said to you that, "Hey, this is going to be my jumping off point?" What was your initial vision and how does that reconcile with today?

Peter: Yeah. I didn't have a grand vision; that's just the bottom line. I felt like this was an industry that had potential and it was an industry that I felt like I could sink my teeth into and get interested. To back up a little bit: I was able to sell my second label printing business, I had started a blog in 2006, I think it was, and it really had grown and developed quite a following, and actually ended up having a large profile within the label printing industry. Basically, that was due to the fact that I had a blog. Really, the sale of my business ended up being really impacted by the fact that I had this blog. I was very much looking for an online type of business. That was my goal, to have an online business and this just fit in perfectly with that.

           I've always been a self-directed investor. I loved investing. I've been investing money since I was ten years old and have really become an enthusiast in all kinds of investing. All those things came together and it really just fit where I was.

Dudley: As you built the community, the community gave you the feedback of, "Hey, let's get a place to get together annually and kind of discuss the topics and the issues and continue to move the ball forward." What was that jumping off point for you? You mentioned a couple partners that came to you; did they have experience in the event hosting space? Can you talk to the growth of the conference from 2013 and now heading into 2017 in New York?

Peter: One of our co-founders had put on events previously, and that was very helpful. All of us had been to many events and we kind of had an idea of what we wanted and what we thought would be a good event. We didn't know what we were going to do. We thought the whole thing would be a complete failure. Well, I knew I'd get at least fifty or seventy-five people because that's, you know, I knew I'd get the readers from my blog, but I didn't know if we'd actually be able to break even or make money. It was a just a "give it a try and see what happens" kind of thing.

Which is what we did and we ended up doing much better than we expected. We sold out the conference, and we just had a great experience. We had 350 people at the first one. It was really a space that was designed for about 225 people. It was pretty tight for that first event and since then we've grown from 350; we went to 1,000 people in San Francisco in 2014. We went to 2,500 people in New York in 2015. 3,600 people in San Francisco in 2016, and we are hoping and expecting 5,000 people in New York in March of 2017.

Dudley: As a participant in the LendIt conferences, it is
            fascinating to see the growth. In terms of the
            sponsorships, how has that side grown? Perhaps
            there were some challenges to begin, and now for
            the upcoming LendIt I'm sure you have a ton of
            interest from sponsors, and I'm sure that has grown
            in parallel with the industry, but can you talk to that
            side of it?

Peter: The original conference, I really leveraged my
            personal relationships. We reached out to all the
            platforms. We got Lending Club and Prosper on
            board as sponsors. So far it was their first event
            they'd every sponsored. I really put a lot of effort
            into developing those relationships and that's where
            it paid off. Now, again, we'd obviously never run a
            conference. They didn't know whether to trust me
            or not, but we ended up putting on a good event
            and everyone was happy. Now, we've got twenty-
            four full-time sales reps.

            This year, what's happened is, we still have the
            platforms coming because they really want to boost
            themselves as leaders and we also now have a range
            of service providers. Because you bring a whole
            bunch of platforms together, investors together,
            you're going to attract the service providers.
            That's really become a bigger component of the
            sponsorship side. Yeah. This year, we're going to
            have the largest sponsorship base we've ever had by
            far.

Dudley: Now you've also expanded the conferences to
            Europe and Asia. Could you provide some context

around the growth of these markets? How it's impacted LendIt and perhaps the size of these conferences relative to your US conference?

Peter :   It was funny. It was at the New York conference back in 2013 where we didn't really promote this. We didn't have a PR agency; we just sort of were doing it organically ourselves. We found we had like ten people coming from China to attend our conference. We had a bunch from the UK as well. I really didn't know China. I'd never been to China. We had a lot of encouragement from those people; you know, we should go and put our conference on in China. For the next two years, what we actually did was, in 2014 and 2015, we partnered with an existing conference; we just added our names and brought a few speakers along. But then in 2016 we put on our own events ourselves. That was first time we had done that. That was a pretty big deal for us. We had 1,200 people; that was our first event in China. We're doing our second event in July. In fact, I'm going to China on the third of January to officially launch that event.

China's funny because it's by far the largest market in the world for this industry. You could add the rest of the world together and it doesn't even come close to where China is today. We feel like if we want to be the world leading online lending conference, we need to be in China, which is what we've done. And China too, the lending platforms there are becoming much more than lending platforms. They're all fintech companies there. They're offering wealth management. They're offering insurance and all kinds of different things. China's just a fascinating place and it's by far, as I said, the largest market on Earth.

Now, you have the UK, which is the first market in the world but it's certainly not the largest. We just had our third UK event in—when was it?—October. We basically had—what was it?—900 people there. We've gone from 450 to 750 to 900.

Dudley: So you have the website, the conferences and the podcast. You're recognized and respected as an industry leader. As this has evolved, what has surprised you the most?

Peter :   I think in many ways, the speed at which this whole thing has happened. I feel like, when I got into this, I really thought it was going to maintain it's sort of individual investors, investing in loans. I never thought eventually there might be large investors come in, but I had no idea it was going to happen so quickly and so dramatically. I feel like that's been a big surprise.

And the impact that it's had on the banking system. I'm actually just writing an article today about this very topic. You've got platforms like Marcus from Goldman Sachs. Now, Marcus from Goldman Sachs would not exist, I'm convinced of it, if it wasn't for the success of Lending Club and Prosper. They realize that it's an industry that's growing and it's an industry that's got a lot of potential. So Goldman Sachs wanted to be a part of that. I feel like the impact that this industry has had and will continue to have, I think, has been dramatic.

Dudley: We talked earlier about how you came at this as an investor and you still invest and you post your quarterly results on your website and you're very transparent about it. Can you share why you post that; what you've learned over investing in these platforms? I've observed you use your IRA so very tax efficient. Then recently, you've been evolving into some business financing with P2Bi and the real estate side with Peer Street. Can you discuss your diversification plan?

Peter :   Again, it came from the readers. People wanted the details of how I was doing and they wanted to know where I was putting my money. It's actually a really good thing. It provides me the discipline that every quarter I actually go and determine what my returns have been and how it's broken down between all the different accounts. It's a very useful process for me, and it's one of the things that people, I think, appreciate the most because investors are interested in returns. I mean, some people like the social aspect. Some people like the disruptive aspect. Most people are interested in the returns that these platforms provide. I feel like that's something that I really continue to focus on.

As you pointed out, I've now diversified into small business and real estate. I like real estate in particular. I feel like it's great. You can get similar returns to what you can get at Lending Club and

Prosper, particularly today, and that's actually backed by an asset. I think when the next recession hits, I think real estate's going to be a good place to be.

What I'm doing; I no longer add new money into the stock market, except through my 401(k), my work 401(k) is a target date retirement fund which is a very traditional vehicle. Unfortunately, the 401(k) provider doesn't offer a solution the way we can invest in consumer credit or anything like that. But anyway, for the most part I only put new money into either consumer credit or real estate or small business credit.

Dudley: I guess we should probably say the 401(k) plan doesn't offer this just yet, where you can invest in it, but only a matter of time, I think, if you were to ask both of us.

Peter: Mm hmm. Yeah. I completely agree.

Dudley: Keeping your investor hat on, when I talk to the platforms, they all believe they have a pretty robust underwriting system and they have the risk controls in place to underwrite credit appropriately and manage risk. Now, you don't have that same bias. You do have advisory positions within companies but you are an investor. So with the investor hat on, are these platforms looking at risk correctly? Do you think they're adding to their underwriting capabilities, or do you think they have room for improvement? What's your opinion?

Peter :   Well, I think it's a spectrum. It varies across the board. There are some platforms that are doing, I think, an excellent job. Others are not doing as good a job and I think those ones that aren't doing as good a job are not going to make it. We've already seen four different platforms fail this year [2016]. Now not all of it was because of underwriting, but some of it was. We've got problems at CAN Capital. And platforms that were doing a great job; I mean, this happened at Lending Club and Prosper where they got a little bit too aggressive and they went down on the credit spectrum. Because there was a huge amount of investor capital demand, they wanted to add borrowers as quickly as they could so the temptation was to loosen up their underwriting, which I think they did to some extent. That's back on track now. I really don't think there's much in the way of negative news being made in recent months, but I think in 2014, 2015, there was a temptation in some platforms, to some extent, succumb to that temptation and went down the credit spectrum. Even within the credit spectrum, you know, kind of loosened up some of their criteria so they could drop their interest rates and get more borrowers in.

Dudley: How do you view the regulatory risk? Are platforms being thoughtful of regulatory concerns? Recently we've witnessed some platforms coming together to form associations, thoughts on the strategy?

Peter :   I think regulatory risk is always going to be there to some extent because it's like banks. Banking has been regulated for hundreds of years and there continues to be regulatory risk from the banking side, so there will always be some sort of regulatory risk on the online lending side as well. Now, having said that, we've got the OCC fintech charter which came out. It was announced a couple of weeks ago, or three weeks ago [December 2016]. That's been, I think, a big shot in the arm and it's a real positive.

I've been speaking with a lot of platforms the last two or three weeks, and almost universally they are real positive about the fintech charter. They think it may end up allowing them to reduce their underwriting costs. It will allow them to have a nationwide footprint. It's a positive thing.

From a marketing perspective, there's been this misconception that the industry isn't regulated. It is regulated. It's heavily regulated, but there's no one regulator that anyone can point to and say, "Look, they regulate me." You've got the CFPB. You got the SEC. You've got a whole bunch of different loyalties that every platform has to adhere to. Having that, "Right, we are regulated by the OCC." Having that is simple, it diffuses when a journalist, for example, is saying the industry is unregulated; they're easy to refute.

From a mapping sense it really looks good, but operationally I think it's a great thing to have a national body that regulates and creates a uniform playing field across all platforms.

On your note about the MLA, that's overdue. It should have really happened a couple years ago.

We have it now; that's a good thing. Other industry associations as well. I'm hopeful they can all work together because I think we need an industry voice. When you're in Washington, they don't really like hearing from individual companies, but they will pay attention to an industry group. That's what the MLA provides: a common voice for the industry.

Dudley: What's the limit for this space, what's the capacity for this and what's the opportunity for the space very generally? What's your crystal ball?

Peter: All lending is moving online. That is a trend that is unstoppable. It's a trend that all the banks now recognize. That's what the industry has done; it's established that in the minds of bankers everywhere. It's saying, "All right, we need an online strategy." There's no bank in the country now that's not thinking about what they need to do online. They all are thinking about it and so what you're going to see is a blurring of the lines between banks and marketplace lending platform. SoFi was talking this week that they're thinking about getting a banking license. You've heard rumors, from time to time, of platforms buying banks. You're going to see a blurring of lines. That's a good thing. You're going to have an industry that eventually, as far as lending volume is, it's a multi trillion dollar industry and eventually this is all going to be online. There will be some standalone banks that will be big players. There will be some marketplace lending platforms that are not owned by banks.

The reality is when you look at online lending it's going to be like e-commerce whereas Amazon, they're one of the largest retailers. That's when you're going to see. You're going to see many of these online lending platforms are going to sneak up on the largest lenders in the country.

Dudley: Is the future dominant player in the space in existence today?

Peter: I think about that a lot. If I look down the track ten years, it's very possible that the dominant player in ten years' time hasn't actually started yet. It's probably more likely that it's someone like SoFi or Lending Club, or one of the platform that are fairly nascent; it's probably more likely. Go down twenty years it's highly likely that the number one online lender in the country hasn't begun operations yet. This is something that is going to continue to evolve. I think there are online lending platforms that will be getting started in twenty-five years' time because there's going to be different technologies, different ways of getting into the business. Like today, banks have been around for hundreds of years, and yet new banks start on a semi-regular basis. Often times they're geographic, but sometimes they're offering a different kind of experience. That's what you're going to see further, what you'll see in the future.

Dudley: The devil's advocate to the last couple questions: How does the industry go backwards? What would prove the skeptics right, what has to happen for there to be hiccup?

Peter: It's funny, I used to get asked this by reporters all the time, and I used to joke by saying, serious fraud at Lending Club would be the only thing that could really set this industry backwards. That's what we've experienced this year [2016]. Not serious fraud, we certainly had improprieties. We've weathered this storm; the reality is we've got to prove that these businesses are profitable. There's some platforms that have proven it, others have not. The reality is we know that it's less costly to originate a loan online than it is in a brick-and-mortar store. Can these platforms get to the scale of some of the mid-sized banks where they're issuing tens of billions of dollars of loans every year?

Lending Club is going do just under ten billion dollars this year [2016]; it's probably going to be somewhere in the nature of eight-and-a-half to nine. Probably around eight-and-a-half. That's a decent-sized bank as far as on an annual basis. The big question mark is if there's more fraud that's a real negative. That could really set the industry back.

What these companies have to be able to demonstrate is that they can be profitable at different levels of scale. Banks can be profitable at different scales. You can have a billion dollar a year, or even a five hundred million dollar a year business in originations, and you can be profitable. That's what we haven't demonstrated yet and I think that's what we need to see. You know the profitability is what this is going to be all about.

Dudley: Is there and overarching message you'd like to
             communicate? What do you want people to know
             and the industry overall?

Peter: I think part of what we just said. I think that lending
             is moving online and the reality is individuals can
             take advantage of that. The industry in the future
             is going to look a lot different. Most investors are
             going to invest through some kind of fund. We
             don't have a public open-ended mutual fund yet,
             but we've got two 40-ACT funds that launched this
             year. Eventually consumer credit and small business
             credit belongs in everyone's portfolio. I think we
             want to be able to have this as an offering, and
             eventually in twenty years' time this will be like real
             estate or any other asset class that everyone realizes
             they need to have access to, and I think that'll be a
             great thing. It's a non-correlated asset class and it's
             one that provides high yields and I think it should
             be available to all investors.

About the Author

www.laveercapital.com

www.capdisruption.com

DUDLEY K. BEYLER is the founder of Laveer Capital Management, LLC (Laveer), which launched in 2014 seeking misunderstood markets, out of favor strategies, concepts disrupting legacy incumbents and inefficiencies identified through an understanding of investor psychology. Laveer's guiding principle—"Price is truth."

In January 2008, Dudley bought his first peer-to-peer loan on Prosper Marketplace. While the credit crunch was not a timely starting point for lending, the opportunity to act as a bank was too attractive. New technologies were beginning to impact banking as it has other industries.

Since Fall 2014, this marketplace lending portfolio has exclusively focused on real estate lending. It is our belief that marketplace lenders are providing opportunities to earn non-correlated returns superior to what is available in public markets. Early adopters appropriately vetting platforms will be rewarded.

Offline Laveer funds early-stage revenue generating companies and small businesses through its deal network. These companies face funding challenges like many mature businesses, but the solutions available are limited. Venture capital, angel investors, and banking institutions do not address these concerns. Laveer fills funding gaps and works with portfolio companies on growth strategies, market position and overall de-risking. It is Laveer's goal to aid companies along its capital lifecycle.

Dudley began his career trading energy, currency, equity, volatility and global interest rate derivatives. He was a proprietary trader managing his capital and that of his partners. Dudley traded on the New York Mercantile Exchange, Chicago Mercantile Exchange, Intercontinental Exchange and Chicago Board Options Exchange. Dudley often worked with exchanges to provide liquidity for new and thin traded products.

Additional investment experience includes a portfolio of multi-family and commercial real estate in downtown Chicago. In 2009, the prices of real estate fell, yet in specific areas property cash flows maintained. Attempting to capitalize on this mismatch, Dudley began acquiring property through foreclosure auction in the spring of 2009. Dudley targets value add opportunities in need of renovation or repositioning due to poor utilization.

Invest where capital is treated best.

Notes and links from interviews

Jamie Dimon's letter to shareholders April 2015 (page 29):

- http://files.shareholder.com/downloads/ONE/15660 259x0x820077/8af78e45-1d81-4363-931c-439d 04312ebc/JPMC-AR2014-LetterToShareholders.pdf

OnDeck:

- https://www.ondeck.com/company/in-the-news/intuit-ondeck-partner-offer-100-million-small-business-lending-fund/

Sam Hodges - Funding Circle:

- https://en.wikipedia.org/wiki/Funding_Circle
- http://p2pfa.info/
- LSE – Listing - http://www.londonstockexchange.com/exchange/prices-and-markets/stocks/summary/company-summary/GG00BYYJCZ96GGGBXSSMM.html
- Crunchbase https://www.crunchbase.com/organization/funding-circle#/entity

Nav Athwal - Realty Shares:

- Medium blog https://medium.com/realtyshares-news room

- Crunchbase https://www.crunchbase.com/organization/ realtyshares#/entity

Denise Thomas - Apple Pie Capital:

- http://www.prnewswire.com/news-releases/apple pie-capital-enters-into-180-million-loan-purchase-agreement-with-towerbrook-structured-opportuni ties-fund-closes-165-million-series-b-300376577.html

- http://www.franchisetimes.com/January-2017/Apple-Pie-Capital-strives-for-new-finance-normal/

- http://www.colchiscapital.com/

- Crunchbase https://www.crunchbase.com/organization/ applepie-capital#/entity

Frank Rotman - QED:

- Frank's blog https://fintechjunkie.com/

- Harvard case study Capital One Financial http://www. hbs.edu/faculty/Pages/item.aspx?num=27152

- https://s3-us-west-2.amazonaws.com/lendit/uploads/ The-Hourglass-Effect.pdf

- QED Crunchbase investments https://www.crunchbase. com/organization/qed-investors#/entity

- QED/Fifth Third http://finance.yahoo.com/news/fifth-third-partners-qed-investors-183200344.html

- Capital One https://en.wikipedia.org/wiki/Capital_One

Nathan Popkins - Align Income Share Funding:

- https://www.pehub.com/2016/03/3321929/

Jorge Sun - LendingFront:

- Crunchbase https://www.crunchbase.com/organization/lendingfront#/entity

Krista Morgan - P2Bi:

- Zopa https://www.zopa.com/
- Rate Setter https://www.ratesetter.com/
- Kabbage https://www.kabbage.com/
- Fall 2016 Equity Raise http://www.bizjournals.com/denver/news/2016/11/15/business-lender-p2binvestor-raises-7-7-million.html
- *Women Who Startup* Radio http://www.womenwhostartup.com/thepodcast/
- Crunchbase https://www.crunchbase.com/organization/p2binvestor#/entity

Jason Fritton - Patch of Land:

- http://lending-times.com/2016/02/10/250m-credit-facility-announced-by-patch-of-land/
- http://www.realtytrac.com/
- http://files.shareholder.com/downloads/AMDA-LKYTL/0x0x822086/3ddbaf36-4a9f-4fd9-ae9d-1e30e9457949/ANGI_News_2015_4_20_General_Releases.pdf
- Crunchbase https://www.crunchbase.com/organization/patch-of-land#/entity

Peter Renton - Lend Academy/LendIt:

- http://www.lendacademy.com/
- http://www.lendit.com/